More Space for Architecture
the work of O'Donnell + Tuomey

Artifice

Contents

4	**Aspects of Architectural Design**
10	**Lost in Space**
16	+ Aberdeen University Library
20	+ Kingston University Library
24	+ Shanghai Grand Opera House
28	+ Three Projects in Hamburg
36	+ Future Campus, University College Dublin
42	**Intentions and Extensions**
52	+ Central European University Budapest
68	+ Academic Hub and Library, Technological University Dublin
72	+ Cavanagh Bridge, University College Cork
84	+ Student Hub, University College Cork
102	+ School of Architecture, University of Liverpool
110	**Collaboration**
120	**Ideas in Things**
126	+ St Angela's College
140	+ Christian Brothers College
146	+ Sandford Park Schoolhouse
154	**Watercolour Work**
164	**Living in the City**
170	+ Sunday's Well Houses
178	+ Clonliffe Apartments
182	**Folding Landscape**
188	+ Robinson Centre, Roundstone
194	+ Folding Landscape/East and West
200	**Public Space**
208	+ The Prow
214	+ Sadler's Wells Dance Theatre and Studios
226	+ V&A East
238	**Space, Volume, Structure**
252	+ Tribute
254	Project Credits
255	Biographies

Architecture is not an abstract art. It responds to human requirements. It remains tied down to given situations. Never entirely logical in its purposes nor reliably scientific in its analysis, undeniably intellectual in its drive, the art of architecture resides a little closer to the practical realm of the applied arts. Every new direction in design is guided by memory and experience.

> How can I tell what I think till I see what I say?
> EM FORSTER, ASPECTS OF THE NOVEL

The role of logic in the plot, so lightly questioned in Forster's elegant *Aspects*, is invoked here to allow us a little more space to think out loud, to gather thoughts partly tested in public lectures or revisit ideas first raised in studio conversations. The argument of *Aspects* was collected from a series of eight lectures given by the author. He explained why he had chosen the title: "because it means both the different ways we can look at a novel and the different ways a novelist can look at his work". Asking for readers "who sit down and struggle with the writer", *Aspects* was an effort to reclaim territory from the critics, to assert that "the study of the novel as a form of art requires the mind and hand of a practitioner".

> Buildings are transmitters of life. They transmit the life of the past into the lives of the future—if they are more than mere shelter and more than borrowed form.
> SYBIL MOHOLY-NAGY, NATIVE GENIUS IN ANONYMOUS ARCHITECTURE

This is the opening statement in Sybil Moholy-Nagy's personal collection of everyday American buildings and one of the most perceptive books on vernacular architecture. It was published in 1957, seven years before Bernard Rudofsky's more widely recognised *Architecture Without Architects*. In the concluding chapter of *Native Genius*, Moholy-Nagy reminds us that architecture is a form-giving art. Apart from the satisfaction of a functional plan that answers the needs of the dweller, she lists four aspects for us to notice, to look out for or to judge in a good building. Let's rename her points in more general terms to suit our purposes here. The roof: how it meets the sky—let's call that its profile. The corner: how it turns the corner—what we might call its contour. The base: how it meets the ground—its setting. The access: how it's entered—its threshold.

Profile, contour, setting and threshold; these observational categories might help us appreciate what it is that we see when we look at architecture. Or what we think we see, when we stop to think about what we're looking at. Not every building is a work of architecture—but we can ask ourselves how the architecture operates, where the architect's intentions have been put to work, why this building catches our eye. The instantaneous impact of what we see makes a lasting impression on our mind's eye. Singular images, imprinted one at a time, multiply in the mind. The human eye is never naked, there is no innocence in our experience, we are ever busy translating, reconstructing the view, recasting what is glimpsed in a moment within the wider dimensions of what has been gathered in a lifetime. We retrieve half-forgotten moments from our past to relive them in our present experience—and this inward reliving equips us to look out at the world again with fresh eyes.

OPPOSITE
Profile, Inis Meáin, Aran island chapel.

ABOVE
EM Forster, *Aspects of the Novel*, 1927, Penguin Books.

Aspects of Architectural Design

In the language of architecture, buildings themselves are the lasting carriers of ideas; in this sense buildings are the end of architecture. And in the end, as Denys Lasdun declared, if the buildings have anything to say, they'll have to speak for themselves. In the meantime, we can set out to speak for their beginnings, the means taken towards their end and what those beginnings mean to us.

From the Ground Up, from the Inside Out We want to begin from the beginning, drawing new lines in the air with each new piece of work. We want our projects to make practical and poetical sense in the world, rising out of the given ground, belonging in their place. We want to design from the ground up, from the inside out. When we speak about the ground, we mean the entire territory of the project from which ideas emerge: the place, the people, the culture, the site, the wider context. These are the conditions that form the question to be answered in the architectural project. A good building begins with some inner order, often with the embodiment of

LEFT
Contour, Alvar Aalto, House of Culture, Helsinki.

RIGHT
Setting, Chalki, Greek island chapel.

a social idea. The architectural design evolves from the inside out, growing into form like an organism, an operative mechanism ready for work. Its formal composition results from the arrangement of working parts. *Inside* is a more complex term than simple interior containment; it means being at the heart of something, in the know. It's about understanding the client's intentions, combining the spirit of the enterprise with the useful life of the building. It means living the project, getting it under your skin and then translating it, working it out in the design.

Here and There Located as we are on an island, with limited access to public projects, we've found that we must move from place to place, extending our efforts from home to abroad, if we are to be allowed to follow a purposeful path in the progress of our work. We can't envisage the work as belonging to only one place, limited to one region. We must be ready to move here and there. It's a fact of life.

But, in a deeper sense, what do we mean by *here*? Literally, at this place or position, site specific. Nearness. Revealing the site to itself. Bringing the place to sense. And what do we mean by *there*? Gertrude Stein, the concrete poet, famously observed of her hometown in Oakland, California, "When you get there there's no there there." *Thereness*, for architects like us, implies some sort of existential presence. In architectural terms, this means a search for physical, three-dimensional,

even sculptural presence. In more psychological terms, this means a search for buildings that embody a vital presence. A vital presence, like an animal body. We want our buildings to fit in, to connect meaningfully with the complexities of their cultural and physical context. But we want them to fit in by standing out. We are looking for our buildings to activate the air around them. To resonate with these atmospheric qualities; both *here* and *there*.

ABOVE
Threshold, Pantheon portico.

Aspects of Architectural Design

More Space for Architecture The projects selected for this book are the product of the collective endeavour of our studio. The first volume of *Space for Architecture* included 14 works carried out across 15 years, from 1999 to 2014. It was intended as a part-memoir part-portfolio of projects and ideas. Likewise, this companion edition covers the seven-year session from 2015 to 2021. Fewer buildings then, some bigger, but this time, to better balance this further account of ourselves, we have chosen to include unbuilt and largely unseen projects, like stepping stones set out to trace a path, to keep track of thoughts as they rise, route markers in between the realised works.

We were sitting outside, looking forward to a big fish for dinner, sitting under the open-sided canopy of Peter Stutchbury's sturdily elegant tent. This splendid tent was Peter and Fernanda's living place while they were building a more permanent but no less open house on their sea-facing site in Avalon, a coastal settlement

north of Sydney. As I admired the joinery details of their outdoor kitchen, sheltered from the wind but otherwise out in the open air, I noticed a copy of our *Space for Architecture*, neatly shelved alongside the cookery books, sandwiched between Ottolenghi's sequel to his earlier book *Plenty*, simply titled *Plenty More*, and Donna Hay's classic *Simple Dinners*; and I said to myself, why not *More Space for Architecture*! Simple as that. Here goes.

LEFT
Peter Stutchbury's tent, Avalon, Australia, kitchen bookshelf.

RIGHT
Peter Stutchbury, Aboriginal cave, near Avalon, Australia.

OPPOSITE TOP
Worcester College Oxford, competition watercolour interior, 2010.

OPPOSITE BOTTOM
Worcester College Oxford, competition plan sketch, 2011.

More Space for Architecture

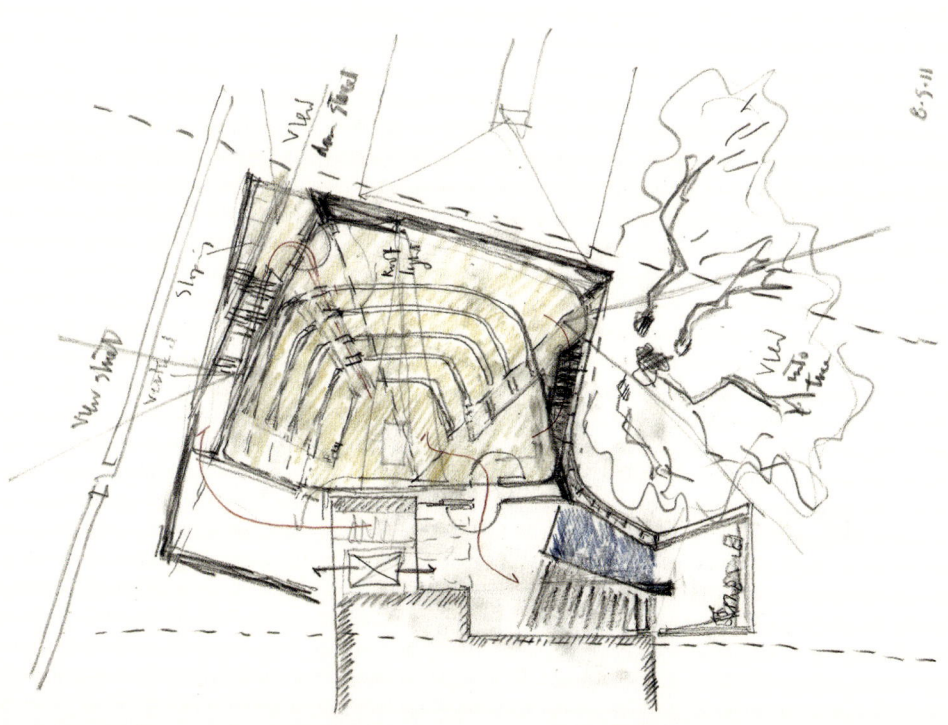

Most of our work, as for so many architects, has been won at competition—but the hidden corollary that must logically follow from this proposition is that so much more of our work has been lost in competition. Gone with the wind, gone but not forgotten. We want to retrieve some of that loss, to look again at some of the teasing possibilities that only narrowly escaped our grasp, like Alice falling fast down the rabbit-hole into Wonderland, wondering if the fall might never come to an end, if she might never see those once-familiar maps and pictures again. "These fragments I have shored against my ruins", as Eliot tells us at the end of *The Waste Land*.

Those wasted projects may be lost in space, but they live on in the mind. Refracted aspects of unrealised structures re-enter the atmosphere in unexpected ways, returning to work through later efforts at construction in the real world. Losing is

an existentialist form of learning. You learn how to survive, how to keep going. The chess-playing philosopher Jonathan Rowson says that we can be improved by learning how to deal with loss. Competition, he says, is a companion guide; it teaches us how to concentrate, how to appreciate human imperfections, including our own. Every time you choose to enter a competition you have to remind yourself in advance that however much you might aim to win, you're much more likely bound to lose. Having entered the contest willingly, you've no right to complain if the ball bounces the other way. It might just as well, and by the same unreliable element of chance, have come to you on another day.

Architects enter their work into open and invited competition for many reasons, the prime motivation being the temptingly distant, or near enough to be distracting, hope of landing the job. But the direct incentive is just one of many factors to consider in this strange, sometimes self-deluding and long-established tradition.

OPPOSITE
Trinity College Dublin, Pearse Street Development Plan, Business School, 2006.

ABOVE
Trinity College Dublin, Pearse Street Development Plan, competition winner 2002, cross-section.

Lost in Space

Some who enter the fray might simply wish to join in the discourse. Others may want to push a hitherto hidden aspect of their potential out in public. Either way, win or lose, the positive and progressive effect of competitions is to refresh the field.

In marked difference to general practice in other arts and related professions, there is the invidious expectation that architects will scramble to outperform one another, reacting with relish to unreasonable demands for reams of unnecessary detail, with no one stopping to count the cost and with little or no benefit to the end result. This creeping tendency is an intolerable drain on our collective energy, a terrible waste of our individual resource, a draining waste that ought to be resisted. In a well-run competition, ideas and designs can be presented in clearly comparable responses, arranged at a common scale and in sketch outline only. For the client, such a competition has the benefit of introducing a range of choice between different approaches and sometimes even unexpected design strategies. And, for the architects, it widens the range of opportunity for rising currents of ideas to find their outlet into the outside world. For both parties, aspiring architects and desiring clients, competitions break the cycle and provoke other ways of thinking about commonly accepted standard solutions. The competition system has produced many notorious, out-of-the-blue, groundbreaking and exemplary projects in architectural history. Long may it continue.

ABOVE
The Photographers' Gallery, London, planning model, 2008.

In hindsight, for us, one potentially significant point of loss, an early moment to remember among so many near misses, might have been our second-prize scheme for a university library in Aberdeen. Every career has its ups and downs, luck spirals in unpredictable clusters and sometimes disappears out of sight in terrifying cycles of frustration and despair. That large library felt like the lucky break we needed at that time. Its pivotal position in the dispersed campus generated a vertically activated section within a four-way-facing form. Its tower-like stone-mullioned architecture rose out of our long-standing appreciation of the hard-stone austerity of the Scottish landscape. Three years before that unrealised possibility, we had been lucky enough to win a large-scale international competition for a masterplan development within Trinity College Dublin. The Pearse Street development plan would have opened up the long-closed island campus to the city neighbourhood and better integrated the historic core of the college with its ragged urban boundary. Having gone to the lengths of obtaining planning permission for such a radical strategy, the university gradually stepped back from, and eventually abandoned, the whole project. Another unbuilt competition-winning project, likewise abandoned after the arduous achievement of planning permission, albeit for an entirely different reason, was the new-build version of the Photographers' Gallery in Soho, still a special project in the rear-view mirror. These painful failures to make the final cut or to clear the crucial jump from concept into concrete reality, are now long ago and far away. A few fresh lesions linger nearer the surface, and some of these wounds are smarting still.

The grand opera in Shanghai was always going to be a long shot, a huge project made to seem smaller by its distance far away, like the cows outside the caravan in *Father Ted*. Having first been selected by the architectural jury, then having to settle for second place in the final round of the political jury made it seem tantalisingly close. One memorable day-trip to the Garden of the Humble Administrator in Suzhou almost made the outing worth the journey. We wanted to make a new sort of Chinese garden, a wandering public parkland alongside a bend in the river in Shanghai. Our proposal was to be a *City of Opera*, a cultural cluster made out of Chinese brick, the indigenous building material once so prevalent in Shanghai, a material that some say might even have originated in China.

Two years of three quite separate but almost consecutive two-stage competitions in downtown Hamburg was a gruelling and betimes exhausting experience. Those closely run runner-up projects, each one lying close to the next on special sites around the city centre, are published here to bear witness to our appreciation for the way the grand commercial buildings come down to hit solid ground in that resolutely handsome and brick-built Hanseatic city.

The first attempt was a big office building in the HafenCity, facing the park and the river. It was to be a new headquarters for the publishing house Gruner + Jahr. We wanted to open up the office building to the city, with open courts and archways in the Hamburg tradition. The second of our Hamburg competitions was at Nikolai Insel, in the very centre of the original port city, on the river quays, beside the oldest bridge in Hamburg and in between the spires of the city skyline. The brief asked for each of two options to be considered, how to integrate an already much-altered existing banking building or whether to replace it with new apartments. The third of our Hamburg projects was another very closely run thing. The site was on a crucial corner between the river Elbe and the market square, the war-damaged church tower of St Nikolai and the busy Willy Brandt Strasse. Our project emphasised the corner condition. Like the first, this last competition came down to a final round between two schemes, a third stage in a two-stage competition, and, once again, we came very

LEFT
Garden of the Humble Administrator, Suzhou, China.

RIGHT
Hamburg, *Chilehaus*, 1924.

Lost in Space

close, but not close enough. We once heard a story about an architect leaving Gottfried Böhm's office in Cologne to seek his fortune in Hamburg. When asked what he might expect from his change of scene to this more northern city, Bohm gave a pithy warning: *Hamburg?... cold shower!*

The so-called *Future Campus* competition for University College Dublin brought us into further collaboration with established colleagues at Allies and Morrison for the masterplan, and newly together with two younger *émigré* Irish architectural partnerships, *Superposition* and *Plattenbaustudio*, who between them took charge of the infrastructure/acupuncture aspects of our far-reaching and rigorously researched campus strategy. At the centre of a reimagined urban plan for Belfield, a college

LEFT
La Loge Theatre, Paris, competition design, 2018.

RIGHT
Johns Hopkins University, Student Centre, competition runner-up, 2020.

campus at the scale of a good-sized town, we proposed a bare-naked bone structure to contain a new school of architecture, a new home for our own old school, an object lesson in non-object-based architecture. A didactic structure admittedly, but a straightforward design intended to demonstrate some basic principles of civic presence and campus continuity. The competition jury report told us straight that they thought our design was not a landmark, when an iconic structure was a stated purpose of the brief. We thought we had proposed a beacon for Belfield; we should have sent it out in a different dress.

In the centre of Paris, as part of a complex urban development proposal, we designed a new theatre, a permanent home for *La Loge*, an ambitious and emerging force in the French performing arts scene. The idea was to structure three differently sized, acoustically isolated black boxes in a vertical arrangement on a tightly controlled urban site. With the fixed and functional spaces stacked in place, and their backstage requirements housed within a restricted planning envelope, we worked with the sculptural volume of the space in between, between the performance and the audience, between backstage and front-of-house, between street and sky, between the special theatrical event and the everyday theatre of the city. The building was to be built with massive limestone, a cut-stone fun-palace to match the material character of Parisian boulevards. The entire competition entry was eliminated at the last minute by the city authorities, for reasons that are hard to explain and even more difficult to understand. Our frustration was to have worked up the proposal in a collaborative relationship with Lyon-based friends in *Link Architectes*, with Paris-based developers and theatre practitioners at *La Loge*, only to have it cast aside unreasonably, just days before it could have been properly considered, and then perhaps more reasonably cast aside, or possibly even chosen by the jury of experts and public representatives.

At Johns Hopkins in Baltimore, USA, the University asked for a scheme to pull their student activity out from an introverted campus and into closer contact with the informal street life of the local neighbourhood. This was a doubly difficult project for us, because the project involved the demolition of a good building by our good friends Tod Williams and Billie Tsien. Having obtained the prior blessing of these site-sensitive architects, whose land-based contour-integrated courtyard was now considered too closed off from its urban surroundings, we worked on this design for four long months through the early stages of the coronavirus lockdown. We would have wrapped the building closely around the edges of the site. We wanted to set up a new meeting place at the academic threshold, a Janus-type project facing two ways, making connections between town and gown, with two white stone porticos to welcome allcomers with open arms. The building was intended to speak back to the brick and stone architecture of the campus and the street-facing verandas of Baltimore. The old brick barn that predates the University, now thriving as the college theatre workshop, was held tight within the shell of our site-specific proposition.

Such stinging regrets have to be set against recent and significant gains made from participation in other competitions at home and abroad. At our latest count, 22 out of 30 completed public buildings have been won at competition. A sustained career in architecture depends on a combination of factors, a heady cocktail of vital ingredients: an indispensable tenacity, a little talent, some degree of dogged optimism—and a considerable component of luck and timing, let's call it timely good fortune.

The cascade of sore losses listed here is intended to ensure that the precarious dimension of an architect's working existence is not inadvertently discounted or blithely passed over in the blurred haze of retrospect. Unbuilt projects are a price you have to pay to survive in this, the best job in the world. Like it or not, it's the price of privilege.

ABOVE
Central European University Vienna, Campus Masterplan, competition runner-up, 2021.

Lost in Space

+ Aberdeen University Library
A STONE-GLASS SCOTTISH CASTLE

Aberdeen is a city of stone, a hardy place made of granite, exposed to the sea wind, where buildings hold their ground against the elements. The existing campus is enhanced by the older structures within its grounds; low stone walls, raised grass banks and sheltered areas of trees create spaces that give a sense of place. The new library, imagined as a resilient tower that shelters an archive garden, is consistent with the character of the college.

The library is a living organism, the heart of the university. The building, planned to evolve with changing patterns of learning, provides differentiated spaces for different categories of users—collaborative, seminar, individual—with little harbours of reading and private study. The design avoids the corporate effect of an atrium. Individuals pursue their separate tasks in a collective flowing space, allowing each person to feel the presence of others.

Universities, in the move away from 'chalk and talk' towards self-directed learning, rely on a greater degree of interaction among peers. Parallel with this pedagogic development is the transformation of electronic communications and information technology. The new learning environment means the library is not to be characterised in terms of bookstacks and reading rooms. Libraries provide neutral ground for students to meet, discuss and learn. Libraries reflect the culture of the university.

Natural light has a psychological value which cannot be matched by artificial conditions of illumination. Natural light gives mood to interior space. This is a fundamental element of our design. Views provide relief and enhance concentration. Brise-soleil and new glass technologies control daylight penetration and glare is designed out. The twelfth-century cathedral of St Machar, located close to the campus, gave us the idea for vertical stone-mullioned windows.

Podium Entry Level 1:500
Printed Book Storage
Work
Office
Showcase
Exhibition
Entrance Hall
Reception Security Area
Podium
Ramped Quadrangle
Lockers
Control
Cafe

Carrels
Carrels
Entry level to Library
Security
Entrance
Podium
Cafe
Plant
Bookstore

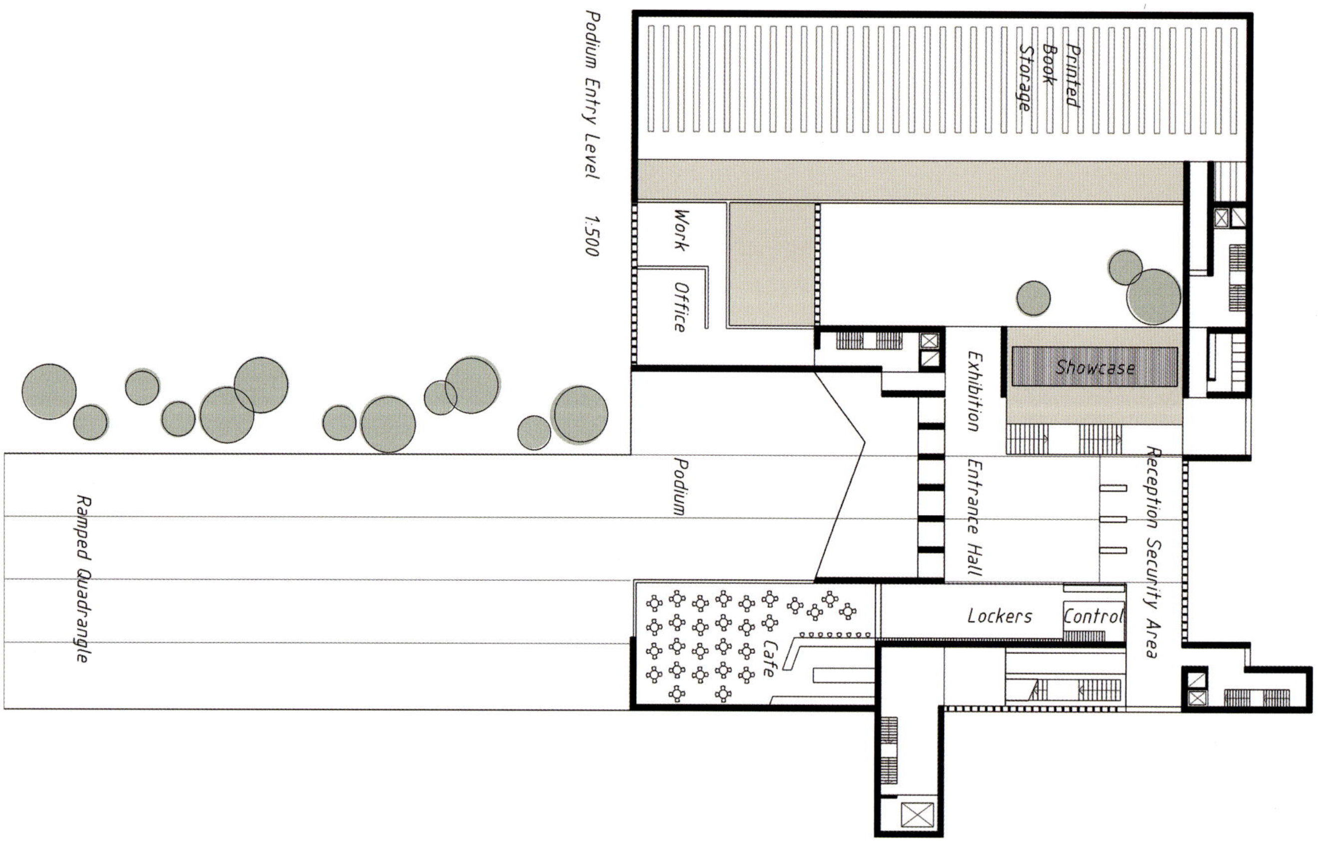

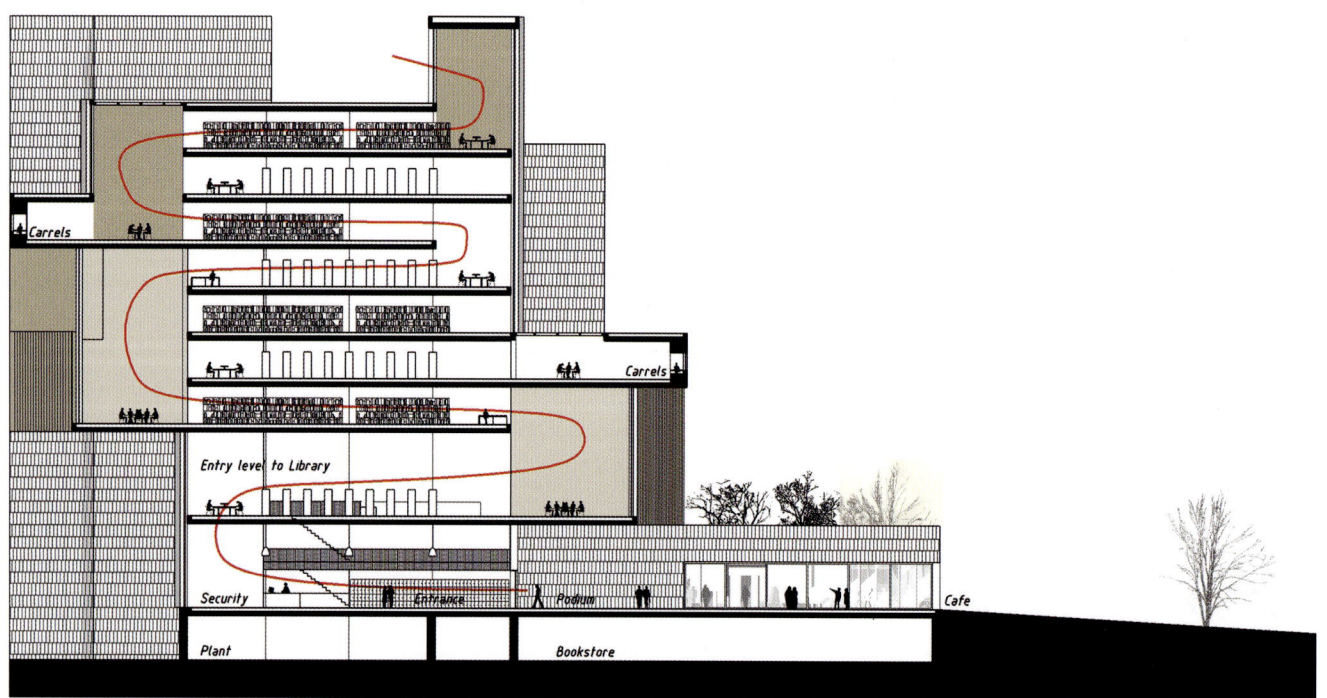

FRONTISPIECE
Night view.

OPPOSITE TOP
Entry level plan.

OPPOSITE BOTTOM
Cross-section.

CLOCKWISE FROM TOP LEFT
Archive courtyard watercolour; Site concept sketch; Stone mullions at St Machar's Cathedral, Aberdeen; Plan concept sketch.

Lost in Space

+ Kingston University Library
FACTORS OF DISTURBANCE

Kingston's Market Place, with its history of multi-use occupancy, was an inspiration for this design. The foyer is set out like a market, a town crossroads to enhance exchange and communication. A light-filled lantern is raised above the marketplace, flanked by performance and project spaces. The brick base relates to the adjacent streetscape. The indented facade creates a gathering space. The timber-screened library provides views across the city landscape.

The building is designed as a multi-level green space, with orchards, roof gardens and new urban perspectives. This sense of contact with the outside world has profound consequences for human well-being, as well as practical advantages for energy-efficient systems. Brick ventilation chimneys rise through the structure, providing stack-effect passive ventilation. Thermal mass in the structure provides night cooling and internal climate stabilisation. Study spaces are interspersed with book stacks to provide varying degrees of quiet and concentration. Like the cross-section of an ocean liner, the apparently conflicting requirements of noisy and quiet activities are resolved within a single scheme. Stairs and walkways, passing freely through voids, give legibility to the spatial layout.

The form is tailored to fit with its surroundings: tree roots, rights of light and views from neighbouring buildings. In D'Arcy Thompson's treatise *On Growth and Form,* related species of fish were transformed on a mathematical grid to illustrate the evolution of animal form. The resultant form derives from the adaptation of a typical organism to applied forces found in nature. Rather than propose an abstractly idealised plan, the design responds to factors of disturbance generated by the complexity of external conditions.

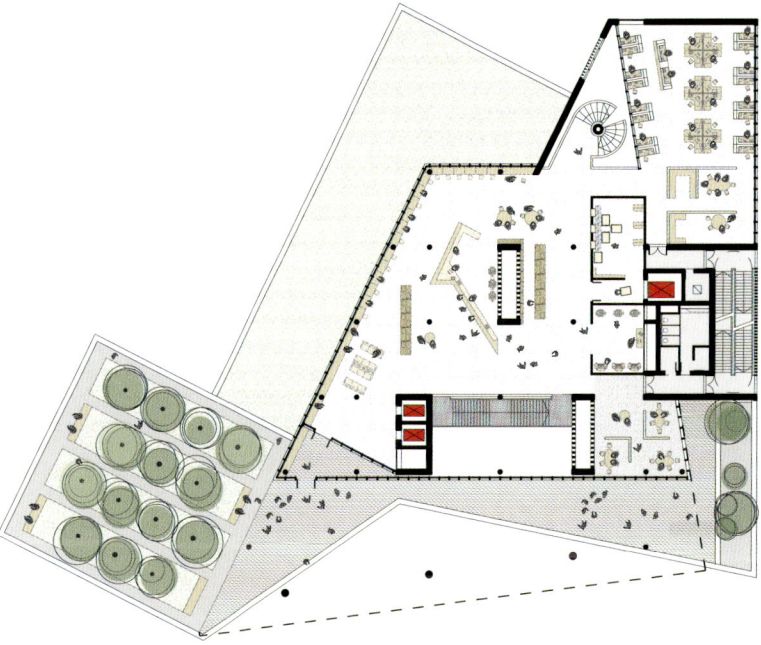

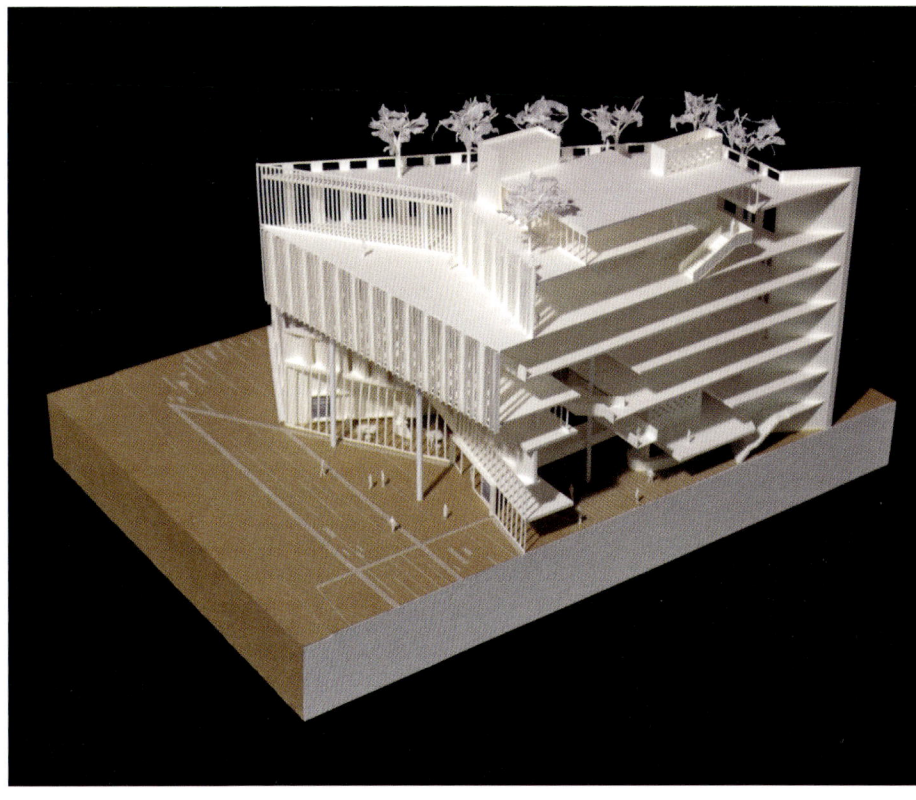

FRONTISPIECE
Street view.

OPPOSITE LEFT
Watercolour, library interior.

OPPOSITE RIGHT
Sketch plan.

CLOCKWISE FROM TOP LEFT
Kingston Market Place;
Second floor plan;
Competition model;
Sketch section.

Lost in Space

+ Shanghai Grand Opera House
CITY OF OPERA

The competition brief was for a 110,000m² opera house, including theatre and studio spaces, rehearsal rooms, backstage areas, library and education, integrated within a masterplan for a new urban parkland along the Huangpu River.

Our concept was for a City of Opera, a cluster of cultural activity, with each performance space given individual expression, each with its own roof shape, with rehearsal rooms housed in glazed lantern towers at the street corners. The defining elements were grouped together in a theatrical scenography, an urban composition to be seen from the park and along the bend in the river.

The theme of our plan was convergence. Building on the tradition of grand opera houses as social spaces of promenade, procession and flow, we designed the foyers like station halls, civic spaces of community congregation. The theatres are arranged as if on a town square, or moored like river-boats docked in alignment with adjacent streets. Public space flows into and over the building.

Daylight penetrates deep into the plan through big light scoops. Wedge-shaped beams at tilted angles admit clerestory daylight and provide space for trees to take root on the roof landscape, a new public garden for the people of Shanghai, linking the park with the river.

Brick is the fundamental material of the project. We wanted a building that belongs in Shanghai, a generous building with an archaic quality, a place of lasting presence. A river-poet's long scroll in the Chester Beatty library and seventeenth-century views of Shanghai's waterfront city walls inspired us to imagine a welcoming place of brick walls and raised gardens.

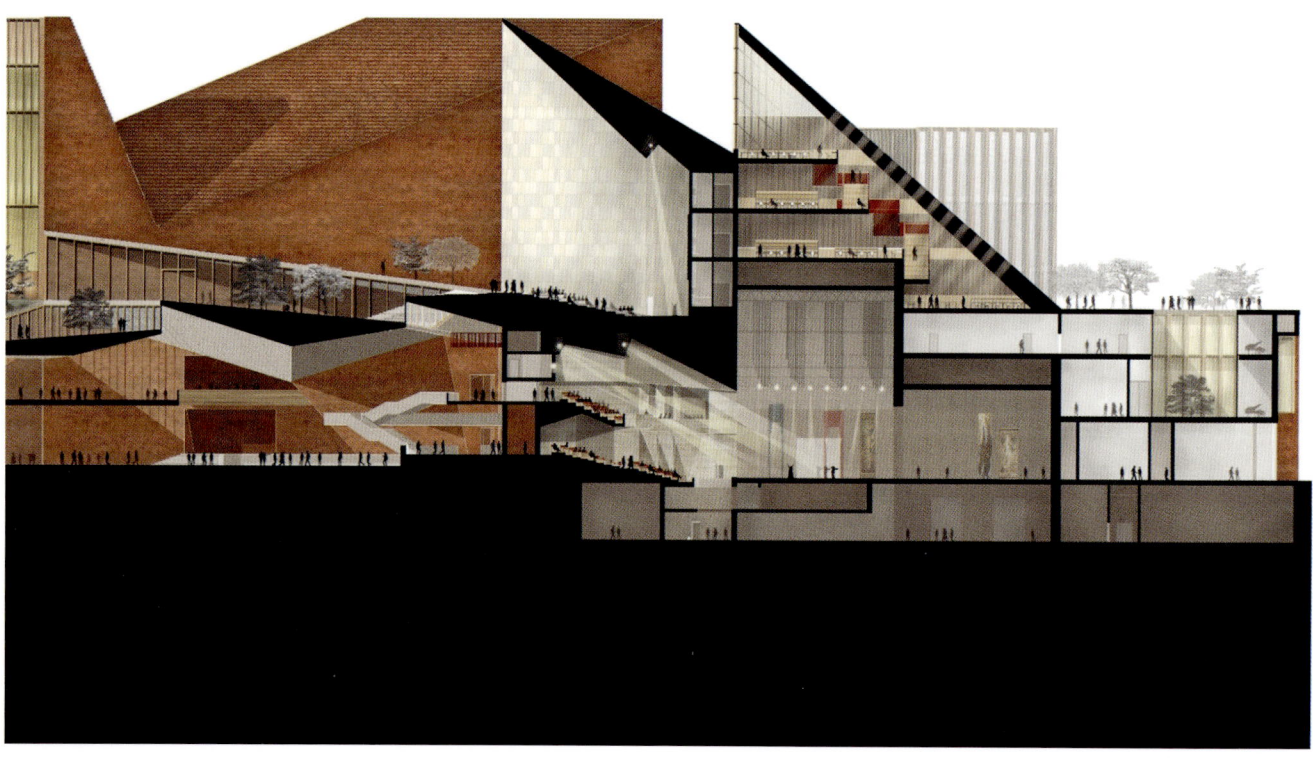

More Space for Architecture

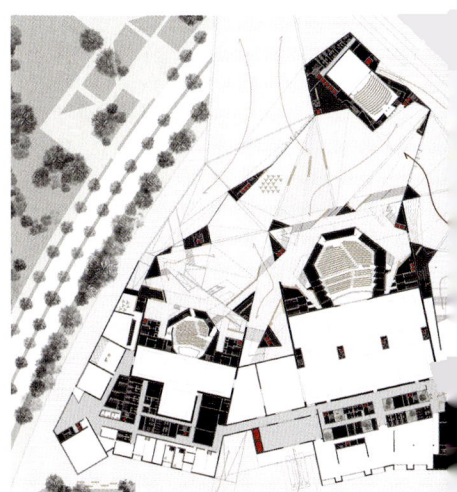

FRONTISPIECE
Entrance view.

OPPOSITE TOP
River view.

OPPOSITE BOTTOM
Theatre 2 section.

ABOVE
Foyer.

LEFT
Concept sketch.

RIGHT
Ground floor plan.

Lost in Space

+ Three Projects in Hamburg

COLD SHOWER

The harbour city of Hamburg is characterised by brick warehouses, civic structures monolithic in form and with elegantly articulated facades. Early twentieth-century landmarks, like the Chilehaus and Messberghof, are organised around open courts. Corners create satisfying moments of pause in the rhythm of the street architecture. Courtyards are accessed through open archways, making in-between zones for social interaction. Taken together, these office buildings constitute a permeable public realm, an urban continuity distinctive to Hamburg. In each of three competition designs, our intention was to situate new buildings within the urban tradition.

Gruner + Jahr The idea for this publishing house in the HafenCity was to open up the introverted massing of the typical office through a sequence of public courtyards. Recessed terraces, daylit staircases and open corners democratise the spatial organisation and modify the perception of an office building. The design invites the city inside the urban block.

Nikolai Insel At the epicentre of the historic dock city, adjacent to Hamburg's oldest bridge, this scheme argued for streetscape continuity in an effort to consolidate pedestrian routes of connection between city landmarks. On the one side, a wedge-shaped site, the brief called for a large office building. On the other, two options were asked for, both residential, to integrate the existing structure and/or to propose a new building in its place.

Willy Brandt Strasse The site is at a crucial intersection in the urban pattern. The rock-like form pulls together the currently disaggregated context and reinforces the historical prominence of the street corner, overlooking the canal. The plan reasserts the urban alignment of the market square. Facades are proportioned like a waterside warehouse, with window sizes diminishing as the building rises.

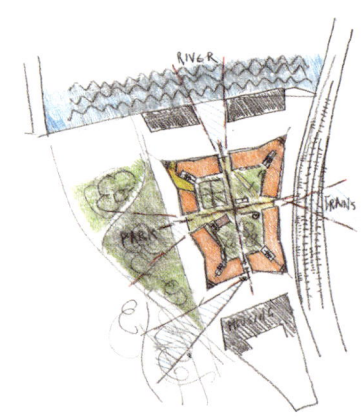

FRONTISPIECE
Street corner, Willy Brandt Strasse.

TOP LEFT
Park view, Gruner+Jahr.

TOP RIGHT
Concept sketch, Gruner +Jahr.

BOTTOM
River view, Gruner+Jahr.

OPPOSITE TOP
Site Elevation West, Gruner+Jahr.

OPPOSITE BOTTOM LEFT
Level 03 plan, Gruner +Jahr.

OPPOSITE BOTTOM RIGHT
Prow, Gruner+Jahr.

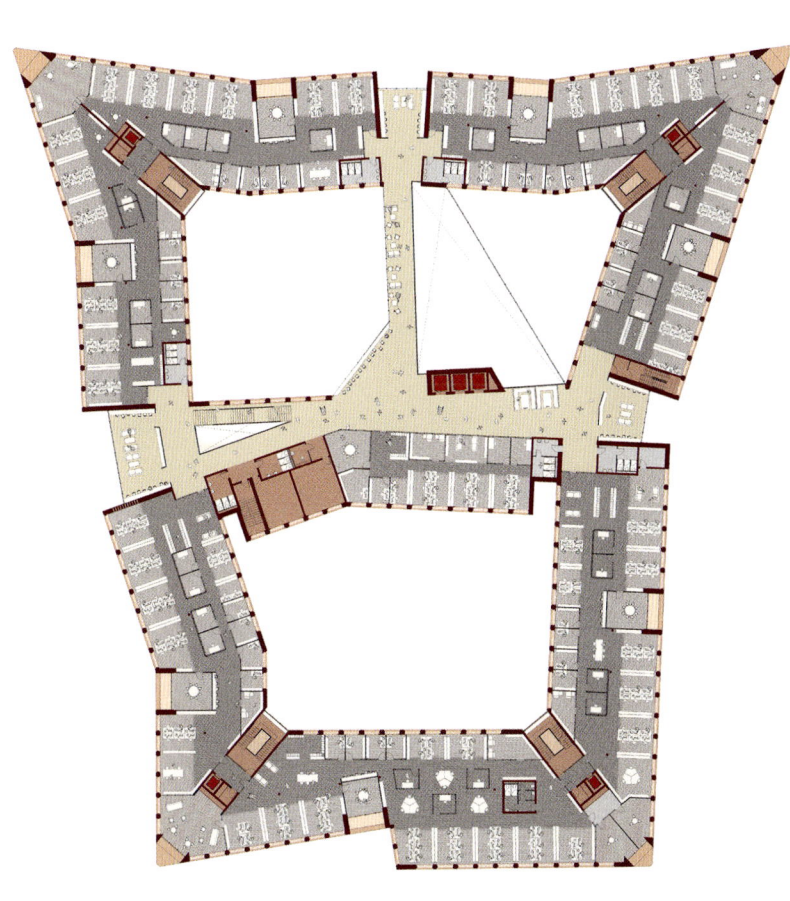

Lost in Space

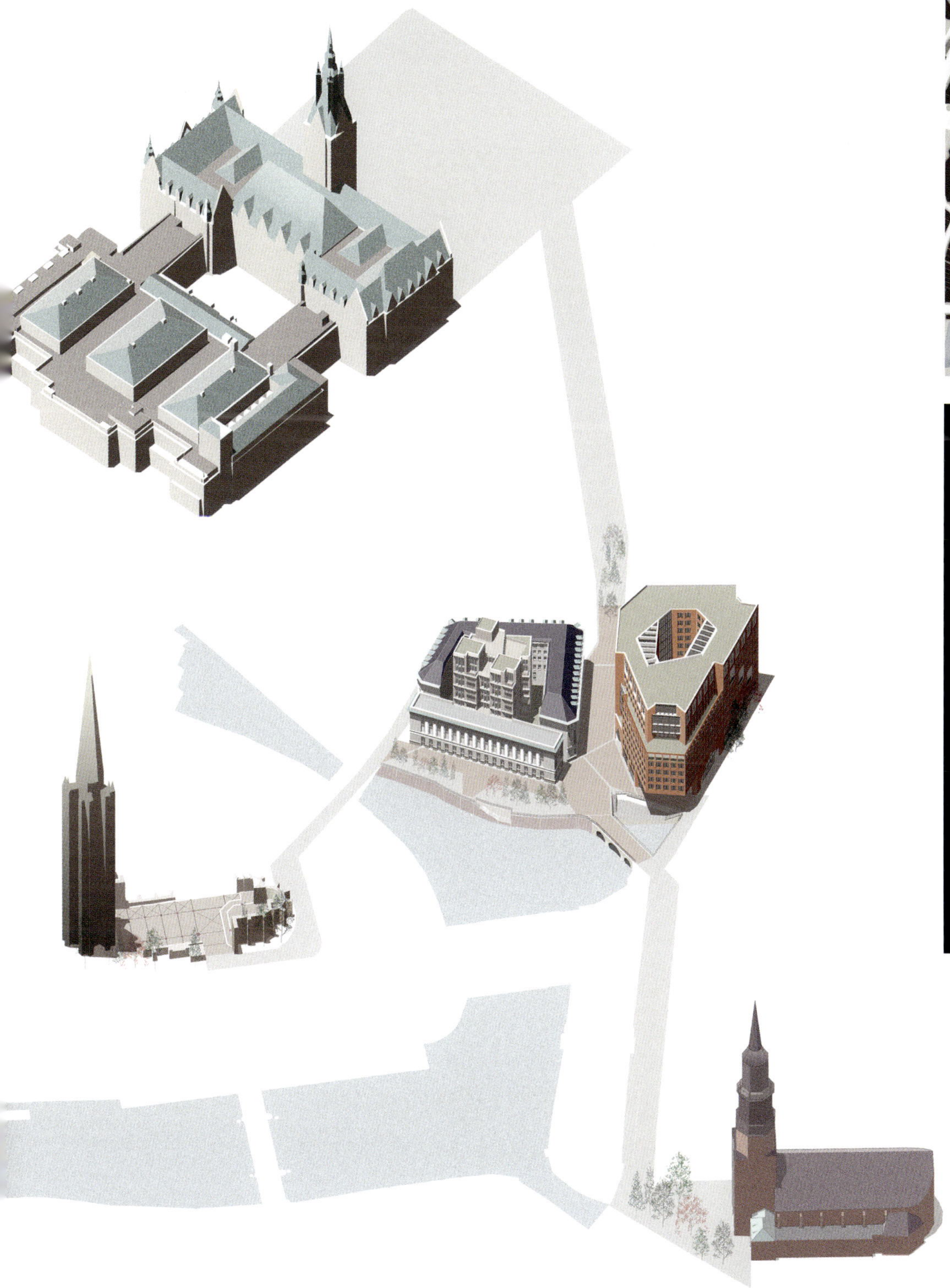

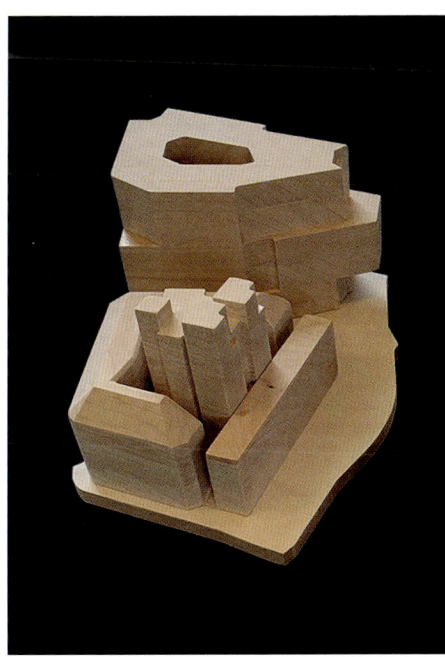

OPPOSITE TOP
Historical map, Hamburg;
Historical site photo.

OPPOSITE BOTTOM
River view, Nikolai Insel.

LEFT
Aerial view, Nikolai Insel.

ABOVE
Site plan, Nikolai Insel;
Competition model, Nikolai Insel.

Lost in Space

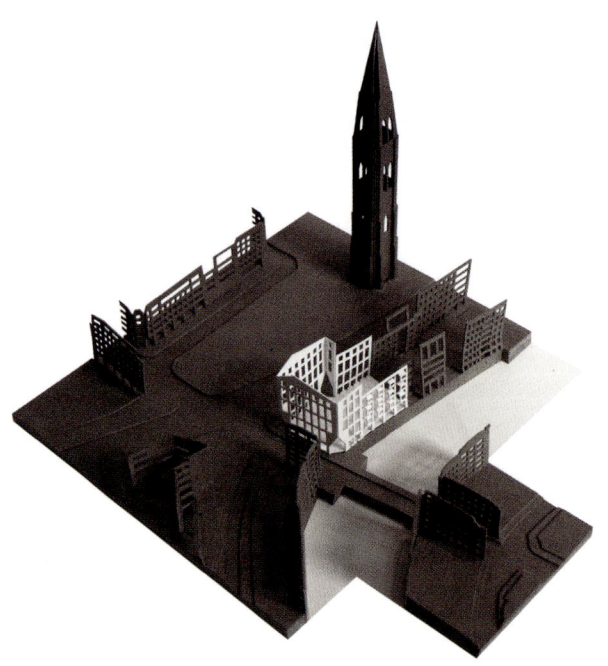

OPPOSITE TOP LEFT
Site plan, Willy Brandt Strasse.

OPPOSITE TOP RIGHT
Concept model, Willy Brandt Strasse.

OPPOSITE BOTTOM LEFT
Watercolour, Willy Brandt Strasse.

OPPOSITE BOTTOM RIGHT
Elevation, Willy Brandt Strasse.

RIGHT
Street view, Willy Brandt Strasse.

Lost in Space

+ Future Campus, University College Dublin

ALMA MATER

Masterplan The masterplan reimagines UCD as an ecological campus, engaged with its context. Our vision is for the urbanisation of Belfield. The plan connects the core to the entrance through landscaped terraces. The old walled garden is reinstated. A new density rises out of the established ground.

Building on Belfield's founding masterplan, its heritage of historic buildings, the masterplan was designed with Allies and Morrison and Hargreaves Jones, with infrastructure/acupuncture interventions by Superposition and Plattenbau studios.

Phasing and Flexibility In the masterplan, each incremental element, each academic cluster, is considered in three ways:
— as a site-specific place that works well, each phase is complete in itself;
— as a contribution to the legibility of the overall scheme; and
— as an extrapolation that develops out of the existing structure.

By this means, every step in the phased implementation feels obvious and inevitable. The sum of the parts adds to the sense of the whole. Each of the development zones is considered as a precinct. This practical model enables the college to focus on one cluster at a time, finished at every stage.

A Beacon for Belfield The Architecture School is an asymmetrically balanced design, a floating structure of glass and concrete. In the daytime, it is translucent. At night, it is a lantern. The facade is an energy-efficient etched-glass envelope. Studio life is on show. Roof gardens provide social space. A new civic realm is created at the entrance to the University.

Studios overlap through interlocking levels. Technology is embedded in the outer glass layer; a shield of louvres with integrated photovoltaics protects each elevation from solar gain. The construction logic and material form make a unified structure, studio culture inside an intelligent skin.

FRONTISPIECE
UCD School of Architecture, etched-glass envelope, landscaped terraces.

TOP
Future Campus, UCD, masterplan aerial view.

BOTTOM
Future Campus, UCD, walled garden watercolour sketch.

OPPOSITE
CLOCKWISE FROM TOP
UCD School of Architecture, elevation; UCD School of Architecture, structural concept model; UCD School of Architecture, section.

38   More Space for Architecture

Lost in Space

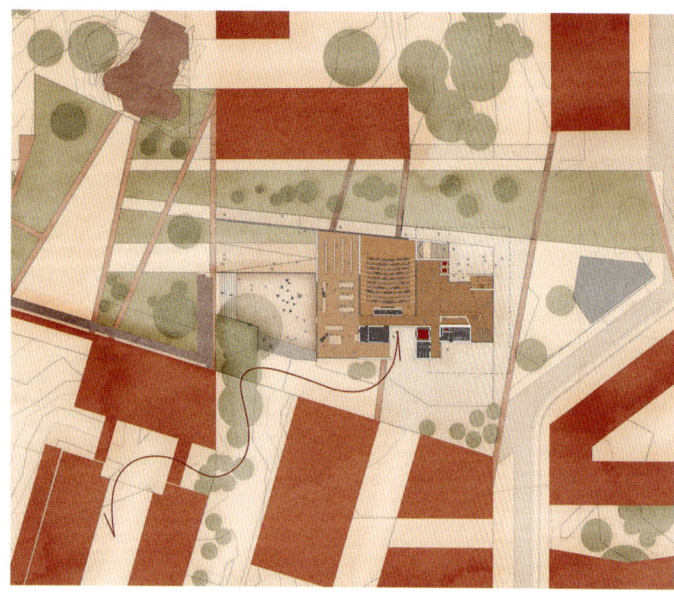

TOP
Future Campus, UCD.

BOTTOM
UCD School of Architecture, context plan.

OPPOSITE
UCD School of Architecture, foyer.

More Space for Architecture

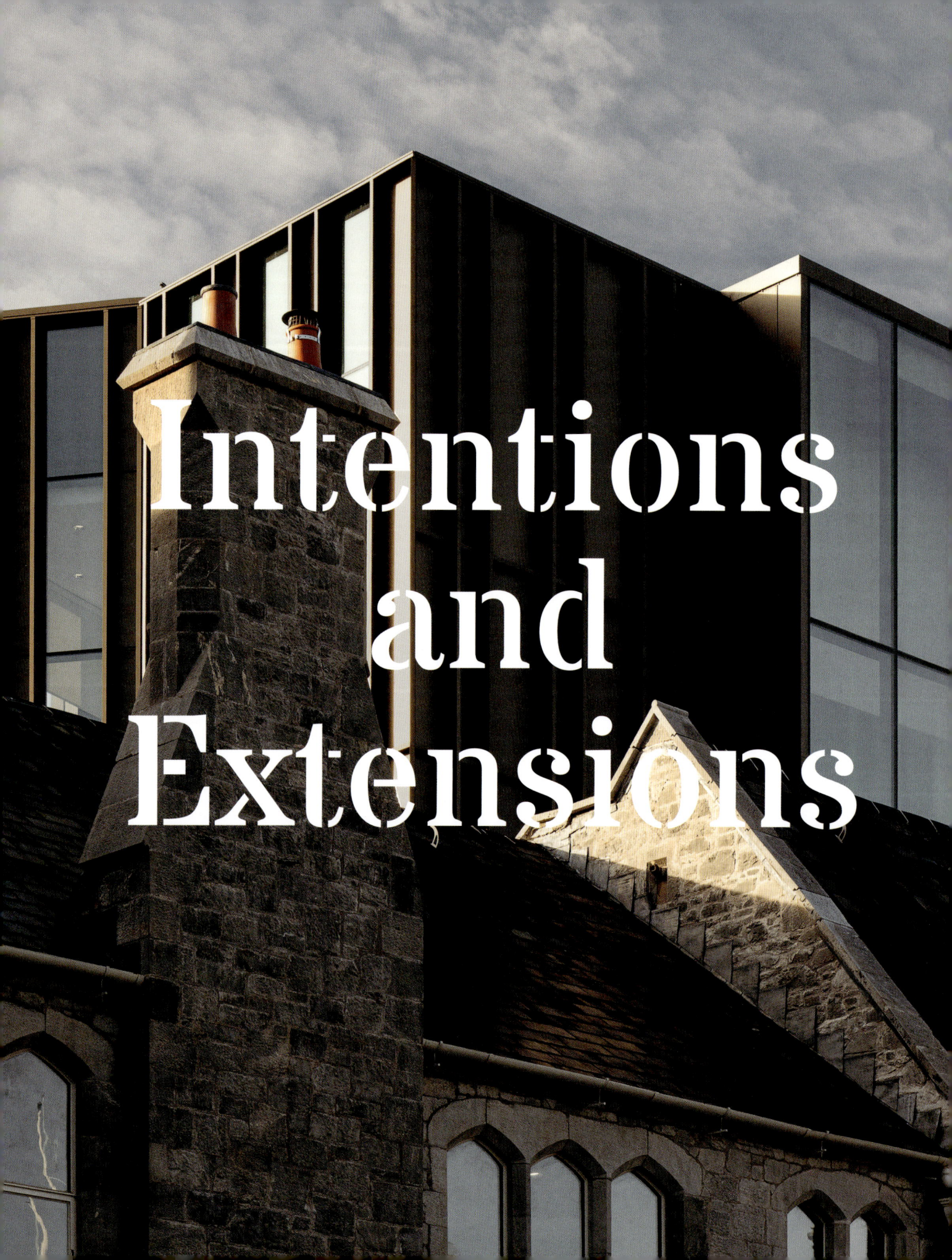

Intentions and Extensions

Some of our projects have involved significant changes to existing structures, spatial interventions in the material world. In recent years we have been asked to work inside, outside, behind and beside different historical buildings in Budapest, Cork, Dublin and Liverpool. Working with old buildings means that each and every fresh idea that rises in the mind for making something new must be subjected to an immediate intellectual and practical test—how does it work with the old? This basic question, similar in this sense to an acid test, being both severe and crucial, pushes the abstract into contact with the real from the earliest conceptual stage. Questions of relative measure and appropriate scale, material consistency and spatial coherence, structural continuity or non-continuity, plan-type compatibility or elevational contrast, are brought into play from the beginning. You can't pretend your first thoughts to be floating free everything must be connected back to the given world. The constraints of this pre-condition are not, in reality, so confining to creativity, since architecture itself is intrinsically tied to actual and concrete conditions. Even in relation to music, surely the most abstract of art forms, it has been asserted that freedom isn't absolute. Writing of theoretical freedom in his *Poetics of Music*, Stravinsky resisted the notion that "art is outside the bounds of ordinary activity".

> My freedom [...] consists in my moving about within the narrow frame that I have assigned myself for each of my undertakings. I shall go even further: my freedom will be so much the greater and more meaningful the more narrowly I limit my field of action and the more I surround myself with obstacles. Whatever diminishes constraint diminishes strength. The more constraints one imposes, the more one frees one's self of the chains that shackle the spirit.
> Igor Stravinsky, Poetics of Music

To follow the logic of Stravinsky's line of argument, such practical constraints, working new into old, might even set you free, freer than standing lonely in an open field. Being surrounded with obstacles forces the choice of where to make the first step. In any case, anti-historical delusions of isolated independence set apart, it would be a mistake for any architect to imagine any building as something out of this world. Novelty is not a lasting quality in architecture. Buildings belong together. They need to get along with each other as neighbours. Assembled over time, brought into being to reflect the needs of their time, they are destined to outlive their own time, to join each other in the timeless continuity of the living present, to become part of the collective catalogue of city building and constructed landscapes.

Conservation and Conversation Working with existing buildings does not presuppose an attitude of passive compliance. Rather than being inhibited by the imperative to protect or preserve, we prefer to think of our work being in conversation with its setting, in line with the origins of the word conversation, meaning to turn over or live with. Resistance is a requisite element in any critical or creative practice. Reproduction is rarely a set requirement. We should not feel ourselves to be imprisoned by history. History has been described by John Berger as "the self-knowledge of the living mind". We learn from the multi-layered and various versions of events long past that history itself is the story of change.

OPPOSITE
Student Hub, University College Cork.

ABOVE
Igor Stravinsky, *Poetics of Music*, 1942, Harvard paperbacks.

Intentions and Extensions

Awareness of context, understanding of surroundings, looking closely at and listening carefully to what is going on already in the sites where you are asked to intervene, can be a provocation to radical action, an action made more forceful by being grounded in an appreciation of its place in time.

> Another great difficulty is that the architect's work is intended to live on into a distant future. The architect... sets the stage for a long, slow-moving performance which must be adaptable enough to accommodate unforeseen improvisations.
> STEEN EILER RASMUSSEN, EXPERIENCING ARCHITECTURE

In this richly rewarding and still relevant book, written "to explain the instrument the architect plays on", Rasmussen wants to help us realise that everything we design must remain open to change. In this respect, architecture differs from other artwork, even from those form-making practices to which it is most closely related—cinema and painting, sculpture and poetry—where the finished works

LEFT
Portico d'Ottavia, Rome.

RIGHT
Gordon Matta-Clark, *Conical Intersect*, 1975.

are not likely ever to be changed, no matter how long they last. A portrait painted, a film edited, a novel published, if it survives at all, tends to remain much as it was, in the way it was intended and not to be interfered with, intact in itself and alive like that forever. Nobody extends a Vermeer.

The art of architecture is not nearly so immutable. Perhaps it is this very practical aspect that makes it so interesting, and certainly more accessible, to our practical-minded profession. Time goes on. We adapt ourselves. We must change with the times—and buildings, if they are to survive in the world, can't stay the same. Since we know we are destined to continue to live in these pre-formed spaces, we realise we have to re-form those same living spaces around us, we must re-make them to suit our changing times. Working with what is given, dealing with the existing conditions of the inherited landscape, is a large part of the task of architecture, a task we would define as one of continuity and renewal. When we find that our own work with a building is finished, whether it's newly made or recently refurbished, we must recognise it isn't very likely to stay finished like that forever.

A simple exercise: whenever you come across a building you don't know, one you haven't seen before, or perhaps when you revisit a place you already know quite well, allow yourself to question how it first came into being and then try to imagine how it might be changed. You should expect to understand the thinking that went into its design. You ought to appreciate its present-day qualities and seek to analyse how much, and in how many ways, it has been changed. Having taken the trouble to recognise precisely on which principal elements this once-new, now old, building relies for its survival, you can allow yourself to wonder what might next be needed for its future useful life.

Learning from the Lookout We have a little house in the west of Ireland, our lucky escape from studio routine and city life. We've made only small changes to its basic structure. The smallest job we've ever done. No floor area added, none taken away, a series of almost invisible alterations, an old stair slightly shifted, a limestone floor newly laid throughout, a void introduced with minimal structural disruption, the whole house opened up to itself, breathing easier as if it had been waiting for something like this to happen. Not the house extension we might once have expected, it makes sense as a house intention.

The tiny lookout is the result of quite a few years of forensic investigation, the question of what to do with an old house of the basic type plan, a plain ordinary old house that had been hemmed in by its previous owners' pragmatic addition of

ABOVE
Caladh an Chnoic lookout.

Intentions and Extensions

a porch on the front and a bathroom on the back, useful both, but not beautiful. We didn't want to interfere with the direct simplicity that we liked about the place as we found it, but something had to be changed to let us settle in. Idle discussions, practical consideration of options, amicable arguments between two architects, all led nowhere—until one day the obvious answer suggested itself, how to achieve the maximum effect with the minimum of means. Demolish the upper part of the problem bathroom block, shrink it down to a walk-in shower, replace a mean gabled structure with a more generous lean-to. Easy does it. And now we can sit comfortably, inside the cockpit of our north-facing lookout, with horizons shifted and spirits lifted. Likewise, the landscape we look out on seemed to have been lying in wait for this change of prospect; blanket bog in front, rocky outcrop to the west, trees lined up to the east, the sheltered sea in the middle distance and far-off mountains to the north, all freshly arranged for our admiring gaze. We read and draw with our backs against the wall of the steady old house, snugly contained within its natural boundaries, eyes on alert as the light moves across ever-mobile Connemara skies.

We came across this hard-to-find place as one happy outcome of our earlier ten-year engagement with Connemara West and the Furniture College in Letterfrack, a community-driven transformation of a former industrial school that was notorious as a penal institution for juvenile offenders back in the bad old days. We have written elsewhere about the frustrations and satisfactions of this unfinished work, one of the turning points in our understanding of the scope of an architect's calling. We tried to tell the deeper story of our aspirations for that ambitious project in a large-scale installation at the Venice Biennale in 2004. We learned some lasting lessons from the construction of those furniture workshops, large-scale concrete and timber structures that Tim Robinson described in his book *The Last Pool of Darkness* as "… quite simply the most dramatic buildings Connemara has seen since Kylemore Castle". The simple little lookout at *Caladh an Chnoic* is much less dramatic, a good deal less urgent in its ambitions, but there are lessons to be learned here too: how to hold back, when to be still and make no noise, how long you might have to wait sometimes to do the right thing.

Campus Connections Over the past 20 years, working on almost adjacent sites at University College Cork, we have completed a loosely dispersed cluster of projects, grouped around the gravitational core of the central Quadrangle. The Quadrangle is the work of Thomas Deane, founder of Deane and Woodward, Irish architects who designed a series of experimental and highly crafted buildings in the mid-nineteenth century, firstly in Cork, then moving to Dublin, and culminating in the Ruskin-approved Oxford Museum. The UCC campus is one of the so-called "godless" Queen's Colleges established in 1845 in the regional cities of Belfast, Galway and Cork. It is said that UCC's picturesque location was first identified by its architect, riding out on his horse in search of a suitable site for a new university—how times have changed. Built in white-veined limestone quarried from within the site itself, the neo-Gothic pile looms out from its elevated position on a wooded escarpment over the water meadows of the River Lee.

OPPOSITE
Caladh an Chnoic lookout, Sheila painting.

ABOVE
Furniture College Letterfrack, O'Donnell+Tuomey, 2001.

Intentions and Extensions

Our first commission at UCC was for a public-facing gallery building, located in the Lower Grounds to the east of the Quadrangle, as near as possible to the University gates. The timber-clad volume of the gallery rises out of a minimal footprint between existing mature trees, thus preserving its parkland setting. A limestone plinth connects the main avenue down to the riverside walk. The Glucksman quickly became a focus for artistic activity within the University and has grown into a crucial venue in the cultural life of the city.

As part of a wider plan to improve campus connections, we were asked to design a pedestrian bridge over the river, directly below the north face of the Quadrangle, where paths converged at an old stone stair at the foot of the cliff. Long-span beams of laminated timber land on sloping concrete buttresses, with each side adapted to its topographical conditions. Archways scooped out from under one of the ramped approaches allow floodwaters to pass freely through when the river is in full spate. The Cavanagh Bridge has opened up public access to the University and connected the riverside landscape outwards to the local urban neighbourhood.

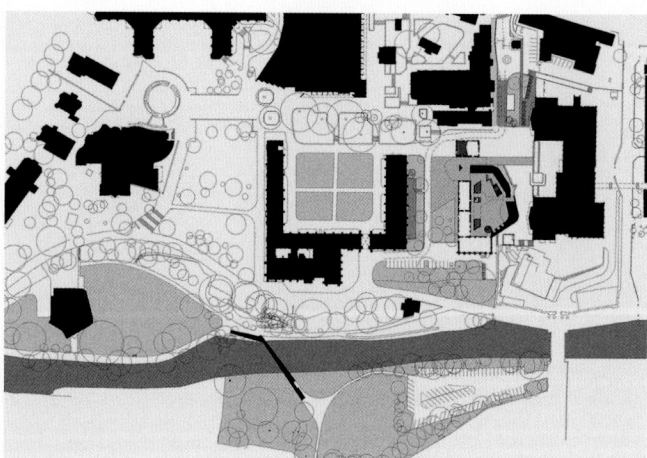

LEFT
Student Hub, University College Cork, model.

RIGHT
University College Cork, campus plan.

Our most recently completed building at UCC is a new centre for student activity, situated immediately to the west of the old quadrangle. The Hub incorporates and refurbishes the 1850s' anatomy school building, extending its linear range with an informal social space for student gatherings.

Thomas Deane's three-sided and partly cloistered Quad survives substantially intact as it was built. Its fourth side remains beautifully open to the south where, behind a stand of cedar trees, a modern concrete library sits in the hollow formed by the original stone quarry. On the other sides, these three newly surrounding structures, the gallery, bridge and student hub, work together in an integrated effort to support the landscape setting of the Quadrangle, protecting its prominence and reinforcing its pivotal position within the architectural composition of the campus core. The three projects combine to act as a loosely triangulated daisy-chain around the sternly rectilinear and static figure of the Quad. The gallery appears to float in the trees, although it is firmly tied to the landscape structure of the lower ground. The bridge diagonally straddles the stream in a sinuous continuation of established pathways, rather than disrupting the natural flow with a right-angled river crossing. In the Hub, a thickened wall of cellular rooms bends around the back of the historic structure, enclosing an open hall for student gatherings, with a lantern tower of administration and event spaces popped up over the existing roofscape.

Looking back at these separately conceived but contextually connected interventions, a family resemblance emerges and begins to relate them more closely together as a cluster of spatial contraptions with subconscious similarities in geometry, material and structure. The plan arrangements of both the gallery and student hub are penetrated by through-going lines of outdoor circulation. The bridge alignment is cranked to pull paths together into a coherent confluence of pedestrian movement.

The three different designs share common strategies; each structure surrenders a piece of its own territory for the common good of the public realm, each contributes something beyond its functional brief, adding an extra dimension of spatial generosity

drawn out from a limited budget to play a larger part within the overall scheme. Concrete benches create useful pockets of pause in the sunshine, and covered porches provide places for sociable congregation on a rainy day. The new buildings act as dynamic elements, vectors of sympathetic change that consolidate the conditions of the given situation.

We had hoped to continue some of these aspects of civic building and accessible culture in a much larger and more complex project for the Central European University, a three-phase masterplan originally planned to extend across a whole city block within the world heritage streetscape of Budapest. The first built phase, integrating two urban plots, one refurbished, the other demolished and rebuilt, creates a new public entrance to the University on the grand street of Nádor Utca, a cliff-like urban landscape where jutting balconies, bay windows and big cornices loom out over the building line, where exuberant elevations stand side by side with more restrained facades. The new building at Nádor 15 contains a research library

LEFT
University College Cork, Lower Grounds.

RIGHT
Anatomy School, built in 5 phases 1850–1890, Deane and Woodward.

Passages + Courts cut through blocks

straddled over a basement auditorium and a public entry to the University aligned along a visual axis with the River Danube. Further unbuilt phases would have provided a public route through to the parallel street of October 6 Utca, and thus opened a new face to the city on the eastern side of the urban block.

The courtyards of five buildings, two old and three new, were to be connected together to create social spaces for student life in this elegant city of courtyards and passageways. The whole scheme was designed to disentangle a highly complicated and internalised campus and to open up the workings of the academic labyrinth, to extend the life of the campus community outwards into the lively urban realm. Sadly, the first phase, opened in 2016, was to be the only completed element of this urban strategy. Contracts had been signed, designs were done, and the builders

were ready and waiting for those further phases to start on site, but politics rudely intervened. After a protracted public stand-off, provoked by the looming threat of parliamentary interference in academic affairs, the University found itself forced to move on from its home in Budapest and has now abandoned ship to resettle further upriver in Vienna.

OPPOSITE
Central European University, sketch, connecting courtyards.

LEFT
Central European University, construction.

RIGHT
Protest, Central European University.

Intentions and Extensions

+ Central European University Budapest
INTERCONNECTED CAMPUS INTERRUPTED

The existing campus consisted of adjoining palace-type buildings, with minimal interconnectivity between them. A selective process of subtraction and addition was intended to transform the disconnected urban plots into an open campus. By this surgical strategy, existing and new would be linked by a legible sequence of courtyards, with research clusters connected by social spaces.

The new building on Nádor Utca forms the main entrance to the university, facing down the street towards the Danube. It houses a 500-seat library above a 400-seat auditorium. The adjoining nineteenth-century building is radically refurbished around a covered courtyard for public events, with a business school at upper levels. Flying staircases connect academic offices to teaching spaces.

A roof garden straddles old and new, with dramatic views over the city skyline. The roof landscape enhances the sustainability of this downtown development. The covered courtyards, with an inbuilt seasonal scheme for natural ventilation, provide a well-tempered environment where local temperatures can vary by forty degrees from winter to summer.

The facade is constructed with local limestone, designed to emphasise the geological strata of the street elevation and to continue the tradition of solidity and permanence of Budapest's architecture. Stone was sourced from a local quarry and detailed to suit the severity of the Hungarian climate.

We proposed a three-phase masterplan, making crucial connections at various levels between existing courtyards, demolishing inefficient buildings and designing new buildings around new courtyards. Phase one was completed in 2016, with the remainder of the project suddenly and abruptly abandoned, just as the contractors were preparing to start on site.

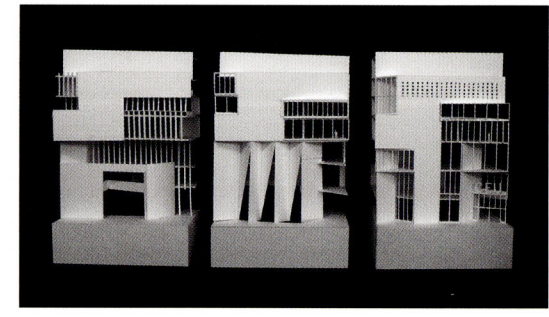

More Space for Architecture

FRONTISPIECE
Central European
University Budapest.

OPPOSITE LEFT
Nádor 15, street view.

OPPOSITE TOP RIGHT
Nádor 15, facade model
studies.

**OPPOSITE
BOTTOM RIGHT**
Site plan showing city
connections.

RIGHT
Nádor 15, facade.

Intentions and Extensions

OPPOSITE
View across the Danube.

LEFT
Concept sketch plan.

ABOVE
Facade detail.

Intentions and Extensions

TOP
Roof garden, city skyline.

BOTTOM
Cross-section, scale 1:450, Nádor 13/11 connected.

OPPOSITE
Plan, scale 1:450, level 04, library and teaching spaces.

58 More Space for Architecture

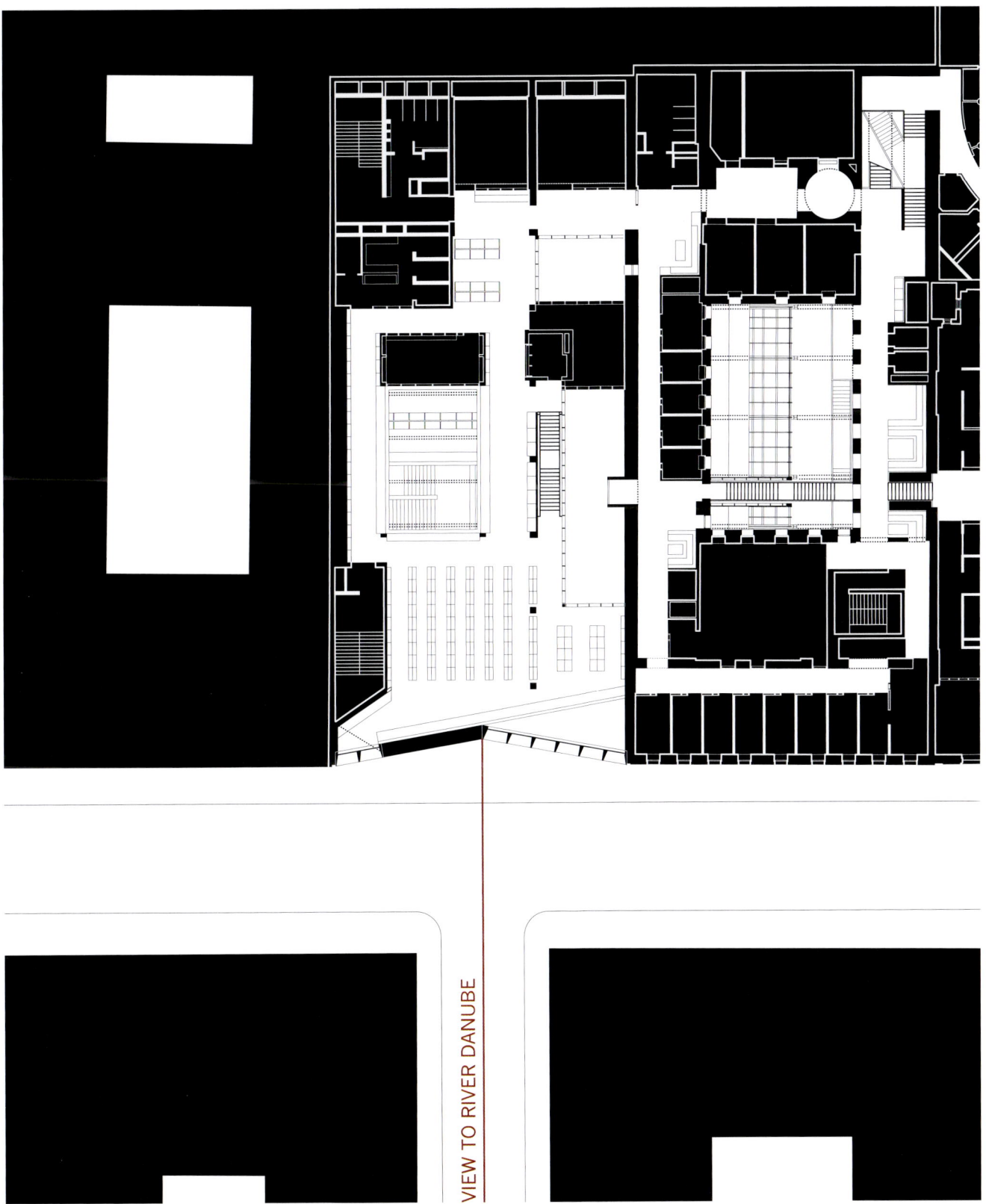

Intentions and Extensions

OPPOSITE
Public entrance hall.

RIGHT
Concrete spiral stair.

ABOVE
Views across internal court.

OPPOSITE
Library for 500 students.

62 More Space for Architecture

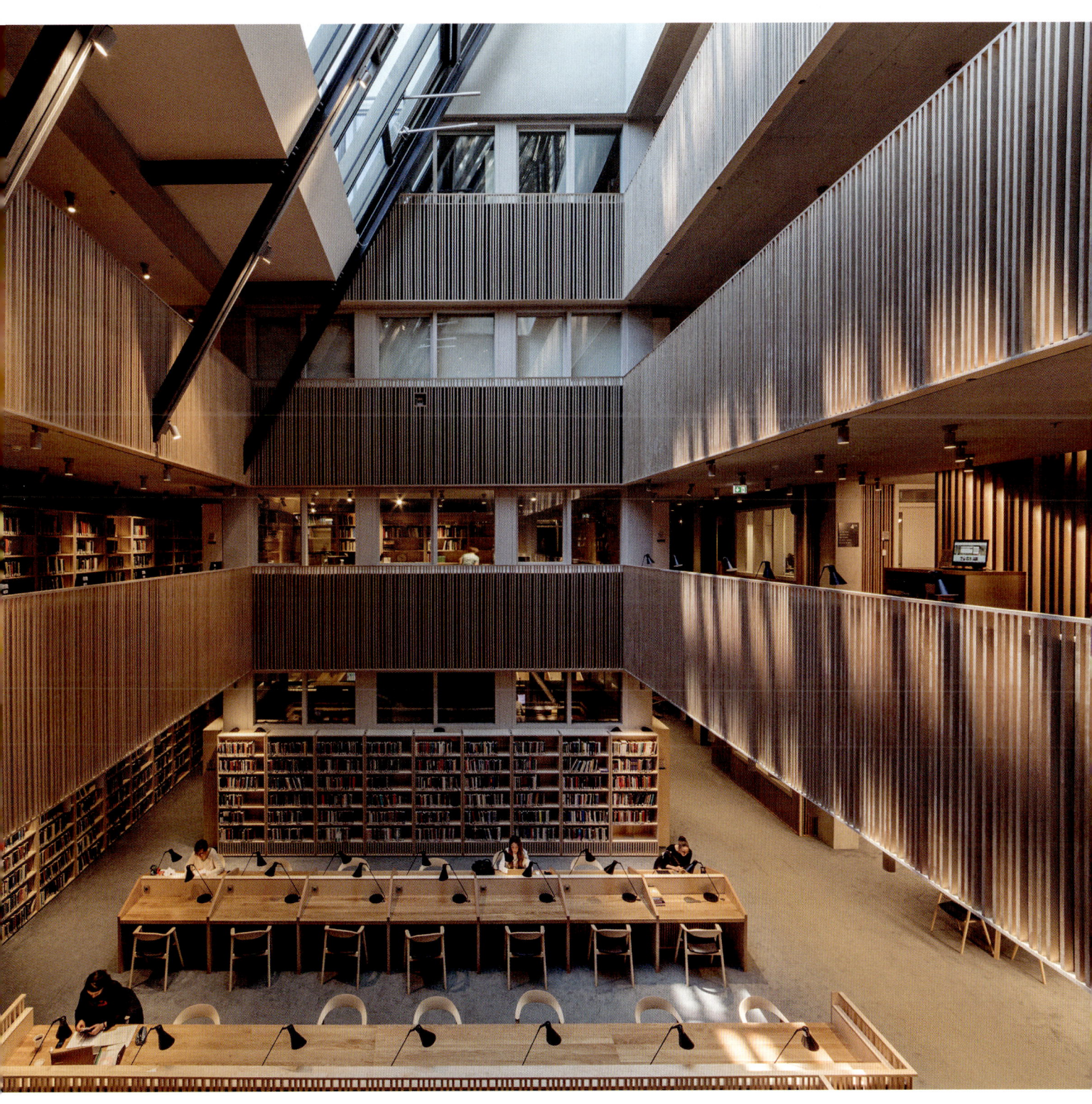

Intentions and Extensions

OPPOSITE
Library study zones.

RIGHT
Library, view to the Danube.

Intentions and Extensions

LEFT
Nádor 13, stair bridge crossing.

RIGHT
Nádor 13, courtyard circulation.

OPPOSITE
Concept sketch, connected courtyards.

More Space for Architecture

+ Academic Hub and Library, Technological University Dublin

NEW INTO OLD

Located at the heart of the new Grangegorman city campus, this project incorporates one of the surviving structures from the former psychiatric hospital. Its slightly elevated position means that it is visible from all approaches within the wider context.

The design was constrained by urban form alignments set out by the campus masterplan and by the protected status of 1850s North House. The shape of the plan, clustered around external courts, is the result of these restrictions. The existing structure was divided in two parts around a central stair and water tower; the three-storey North House West with its central spine wall suggesting a cellular plan, and the two-storey North House East, a frame building with the potential for open-plan spaces.

Our competition design proposed incremental elements, integrated with the scale of the existing, rather than a single large building that could envelop and consume the North House. The cluster concept generates landscaped courtyards and pocket spaces between old and new buildings, delaying the security threshold between the library and the life of the campus. The entry level is set out like a market, a learning commons with the library above.

The library is envisaged as a light-filled sequence of spaces, with views out across the city landscape and to the Dublin Mountains. The cast-iron structure of the North House East makes a transition between the learning commons and the more controlled study environment of the library. Steel stairways thread a legible route through all levels of the library. The project is being built in two phases. On completion, the whole complex will be fully connected in a spatial continuity.

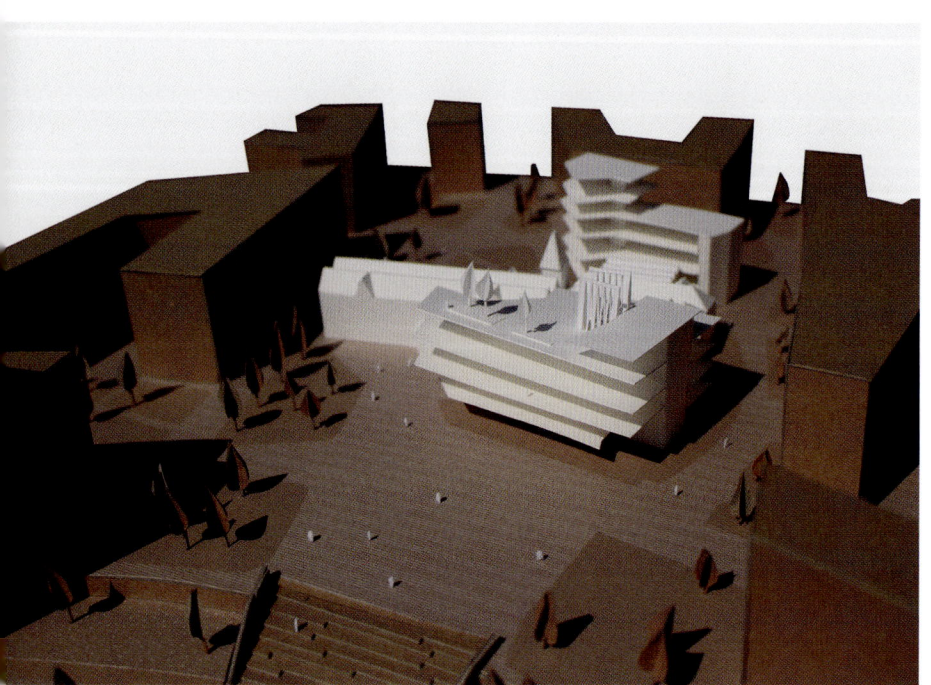

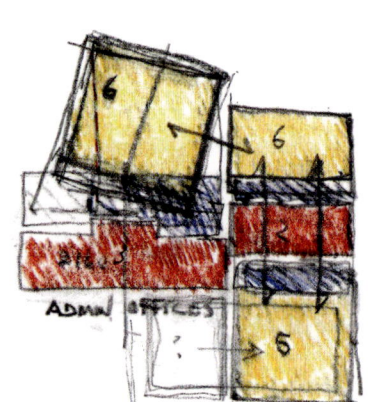

70   More Space for Architecture

FRONTISPIECE
Academic Hub,
Grangegorman Campus.

OPPOSITE TOP
Cross-section, south
to north.

**OPPOSITE
BOTTOM LEFT**
Model, competition
design.

**OPPOSITE
BOTTOM RIGHT**
Concept sketch.

TOP
Library interior, level 01.

BOTTOM
External perspective,
south elevation.

Intentions and Extensions

+ Cavanagh Bridge, University College Cork

BRIDGE AS A VERB, NOT A NOUN

The bridge acts as a crucial link in the chain of connection between the university and its north city neighbourhood. The landscape strategy opens up the parkland on the northern riverbank for public use, consolidates the meandering character of the lower grounds and makes a new route to the Glucksman Gallery. The riverside gardens provide shared amenity space between the city and the campus community. The newly accessible gardens, with changing meadow grass landscapes and serpentine pathways offer new perspectives to the University Quadrangle.

Five laminated beams span the 27-metre riverbed, spreading out like fingers splayed apart to land lightly on sculptural abutments. The upper bridgeway is assembled in carefully joined lengths of untreated hardwood, with each diminishing component framed in galvanised steel sections, and with small lights fitting in between the balustrade uprights.

Cast in situ concrete abutments were modelled to integrate floodwater archways, steps, ramps, walls and bench seats within the structural form. Applied finishing techniques to the concrete, sandblasting, grinding, polishing and trowelling, contribute a tactile feeling to this everyday material. Construction details were given careful consideration to allow concrete and prefabricated timber elements to be brought together in a logical construction sequence.

The bridge spans the river diagonally, rather than the shortest way straight across, to maintain a confluence of desire lines between pedestrian routes. The spatial experience of the resulting structure appears simple and effortless, allowing the word "bridge" to be understood as a verb rather than a noun, belying the technical complexity of its design and assembly.

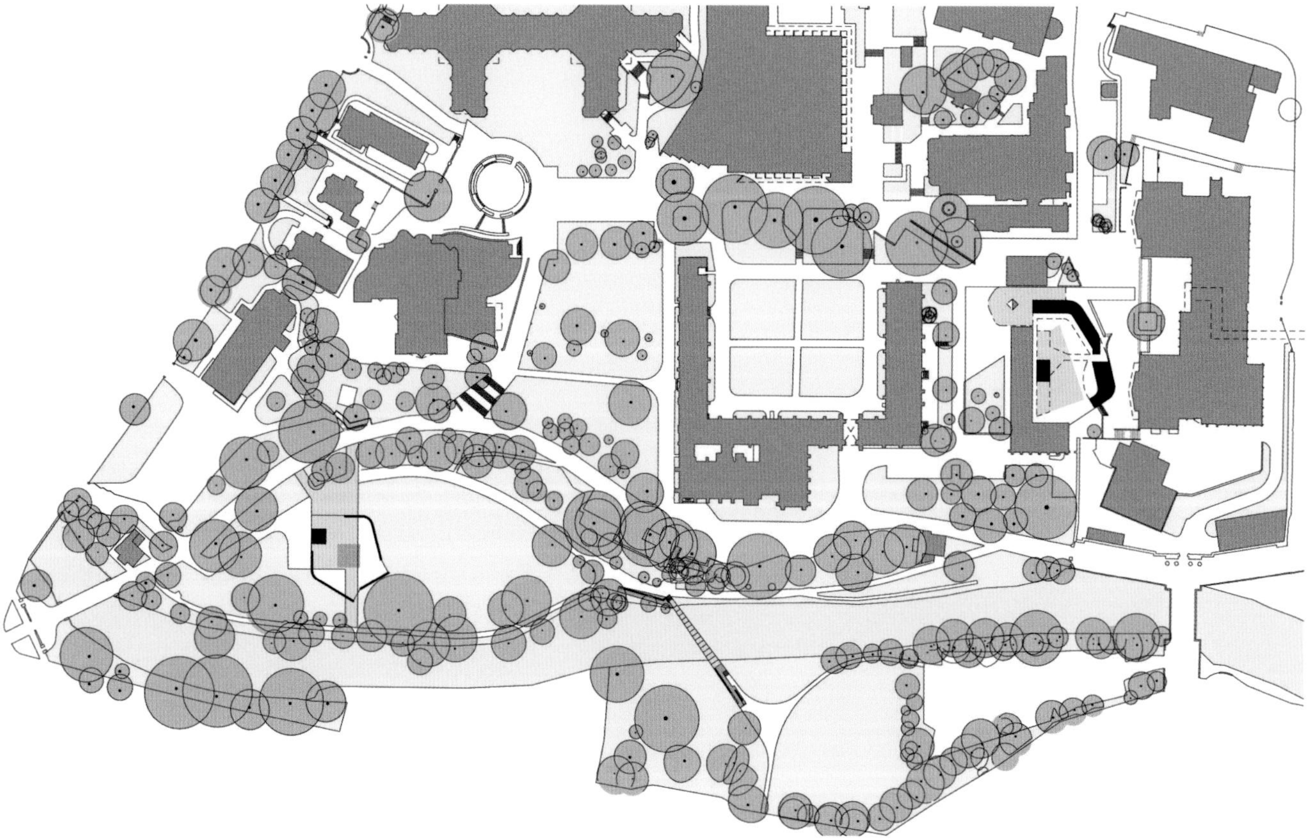

More Space for Architecture

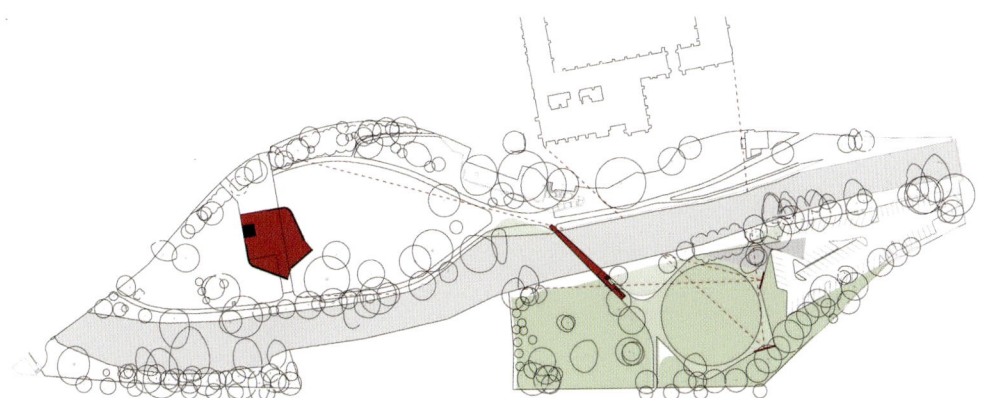

FRONTISPIECE
View from bridge to clifftop Quad.

OPPOSITE TOP
Model.

OPPOSITE BOTTOM
University College Cork, three projects in context.

TOP
View from above.

BOTTOM
Site plan, campus connections.

Intentions and Extensions

78   More Space for Architecture

PREVIOUS PAGE
View from Western Road.

OPPOSITE TOP
West elevation.

OPPOSITE BOTTOM AND RIGHT
Concrete details.

Intentions and Extensions

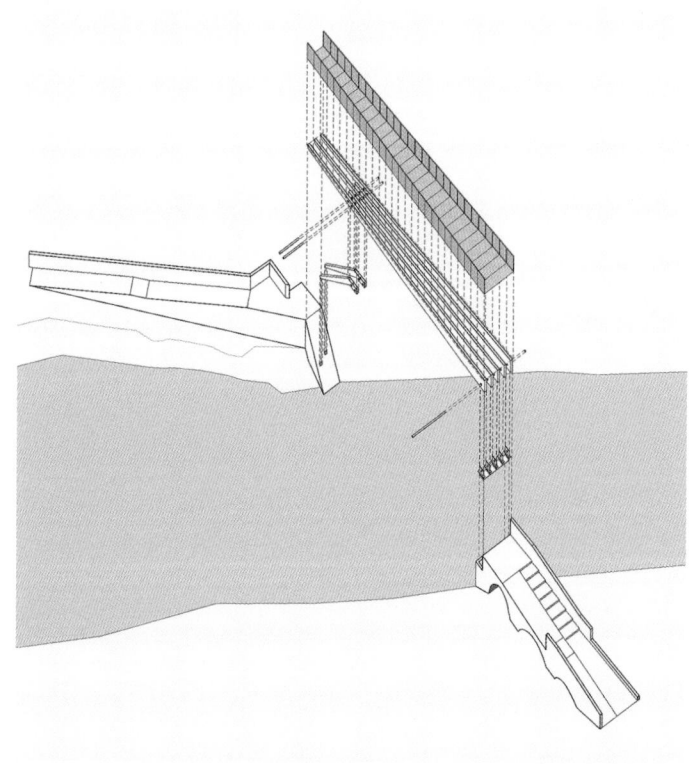

TOP
Routes converging.

BOTTOM
Structural elements.

OPPOSITE
Structural details.

OVERLEAF
Evening view.

80 More Space for Architecture

The spatial experience of the resulting structure appears simple and effortless, allowing the word "bridge" to be understood as a verb rather than a noun, and belying the technical complexity of its design and assembly.

+ Student Hub, University College Cork

REPAIRS AND RENOVATIONS

The Hub is a new centre for student activity, adjacent to the university quadrangle. The linear plan arrangement of the old anatomy school acted as an anchoring element, a strong figure that could withstand the radical transformation of its spatial operation. The refurbished building combines aspects of change and conservation.

One difficulty was how to adapt the historic structure to provide useful spaces for staff and students. The 1850–1890 complex is listed as a building of significance in UCC's Conservation Plan and on the National Inventory of Architectural Heritage. A number of handsome spaces had been compromised through inappropriate use. Ad-hoc extensions were demolished to reveal the original scale of the structure. The landscape setting has been repaired by the removal of car parks and the addition of brick-paved pedestrian surfaces running continuous from inside to out.

Extensive research was carried out into the history of the building. Architects and engineers worked to a scientific degree with building analysts and experts to arrive at cost-effective and sustainable strategies: creative tactics for contemporary conservation. The building form maximises daylight, natural ventilation with enhanced thermal mass. The curved boundary wall is finished in lime render, with limestone window mullions spaced at a rhythm that relates to the neo-gothic fenestration pattern of the existing building. A new canopy leads to a covered porch and open passageway, external space carved out of the built fabric at the convergence of routes through the campus core.

A thickened wall bends around the back of the old stone structure to enclose a large internal space. A lantern tower of administration and event spaces is raised over the existing roofscape, its steel columnar structure penetrating the central space. Bridges and balconies animate the volume of the gathering space, making a "market hall" atmosphere for student societies and public meetings.

The long curved boundary wall is finished in lime render, with limestone window mullions spaced at a rhythm that relates to the neo-gothic fenestration pattern of the existing building.

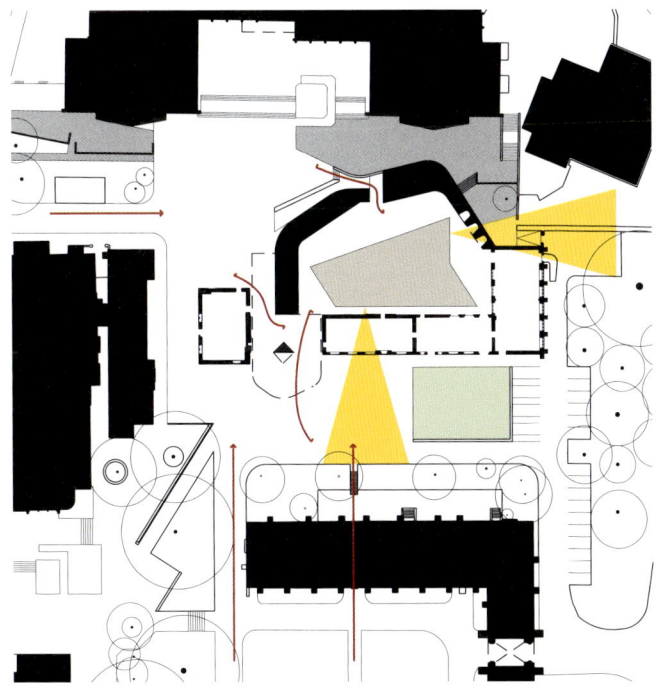

FRONTISPIECE
Limestone details.

OPPOSITE
Congested context.

TOP
Roofscape in context.

BOTTOM
Site plan in context.

OVERLEAF
New meeting place.

Intentions and Extensions

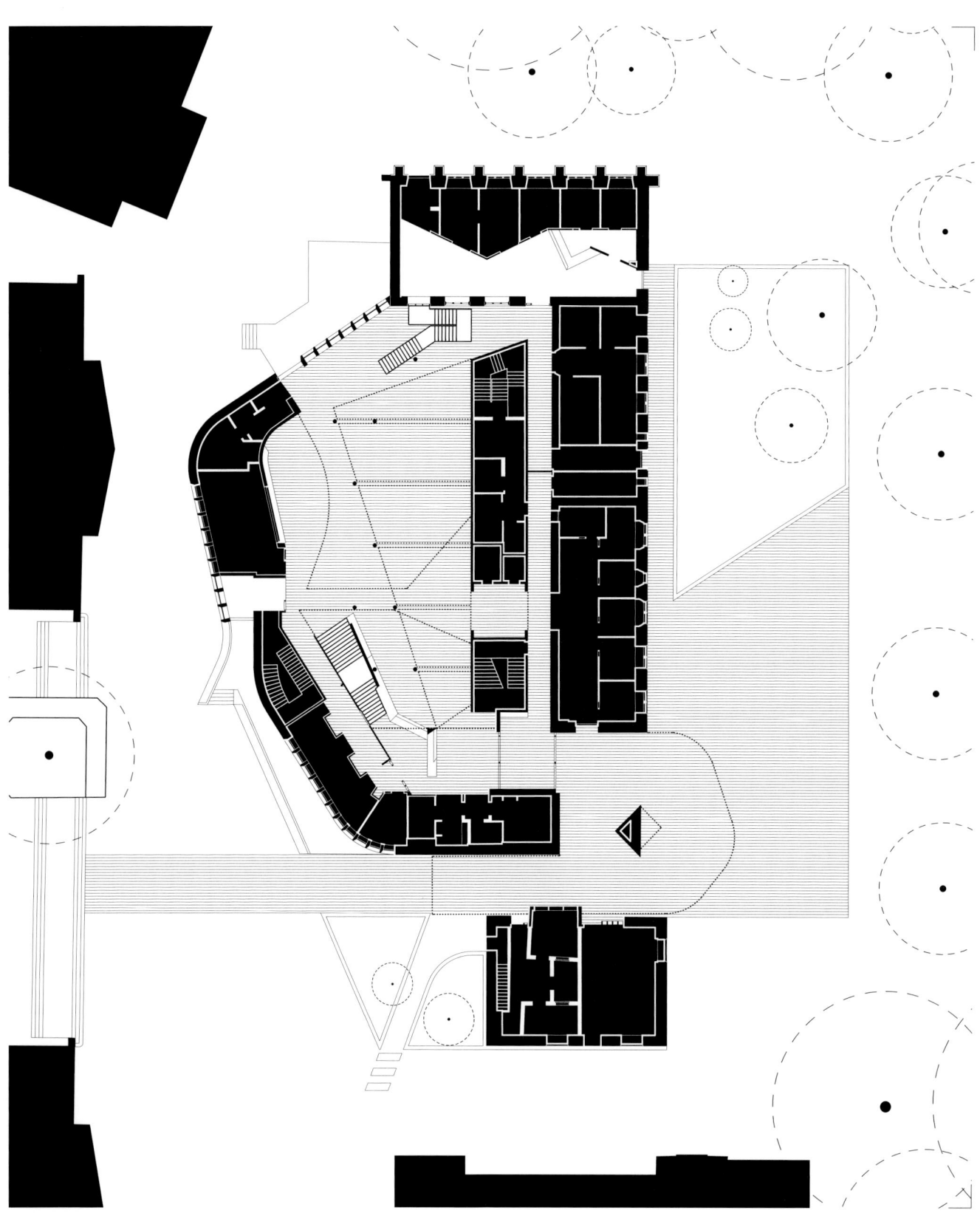

OPPOSITE
Plan, scale 1:450, public passage and market hall.

RIGHT
Limestone mullions and limestone walls.

OVERLEAF
Open frame.

Intentions and Extensions

Intentions and Extensions

OPPOSITE
Office space nested under roof trusses.

FROM TOP
Material detail; East elevation.

Intentions and Extensions

LEFT
Limestone and lime render.

OPPOSITE
Triangular skylights.

98   More Space for Architecture

OPPOSITE TOP
Curvilinear mezzanine.

OPPOSITE BOTTOM
Cross-section cutting west to east.

RIGHT
Market hall looking east; brick floor, concrete walls and steel columns.

OVERLEAF
Market hall.

Intentions and Extensions

Bridges and balconies animate the volume of the gathering space, making a "market hall" atmosphere for student societies and public meetings.

+ School of Architecture University of Liverpool

FROM THE GROUND UP, FROM THE INSIDE OUT

The brief for this unusual competition aimed "to redefine the nature of architectural education and to challenge the current preconceptions of architectural design, imagining a building respectful of tradition, but ambitious enough to anticipate the architecture to come". The School was committed to an inclusive process, involving staff and students in the competition assessment together with an external jury; Maria Balshaw, Kenneth Frampton (chair), Juhani Pallasmaa and Michael Wilford. The Liverpool School, having been the alma mater of James Stirling, was a special project for us.

The existing complex includes Georgian terraced houses, a 1930s courtyard building with subsequent infill and extension works. The brief recognised the "lack of cohesion among the parts, a missing public core and social spaces" while requiring all of the existing fabric to be retained. Our design adds to the narrative, starting from the baseline of the Georgian square, relating to the scale of the existing buildings, respecting their material presence and responding to the roof-lit section. Previously disconnected parts are stitched together to make a meaningful whole.

We started from the ground up; from an analysis of the site conditions, from the history of the school, from a desire to embody the project aspirations. The extension opens towards the angled geometry of the Lutyens / Gibberd cathedral. It makes a new entrance on the main street of the campus. It turns the corner to face the central green space. The building belongs to its place.

We started from the inside out; a concrete table supports timber-trussed loft-space studios above. The gathering hall is a public exhibition space, its ribbed slab supported on haunch-headed columns. Upper level studios are arranged under 30m clear-span roof trusses, with solar-shaded daylighting. The building is designed to be adaptable to change and to last a long time.

FRONTISPIECE
External view
competition design.

TOP
Mezzanine view,
crit space.

BOTTOM
Ground floor view,
exhibition hall.

OPPOSITE
Plan, scale 1:450.

104   More Space for Architecture

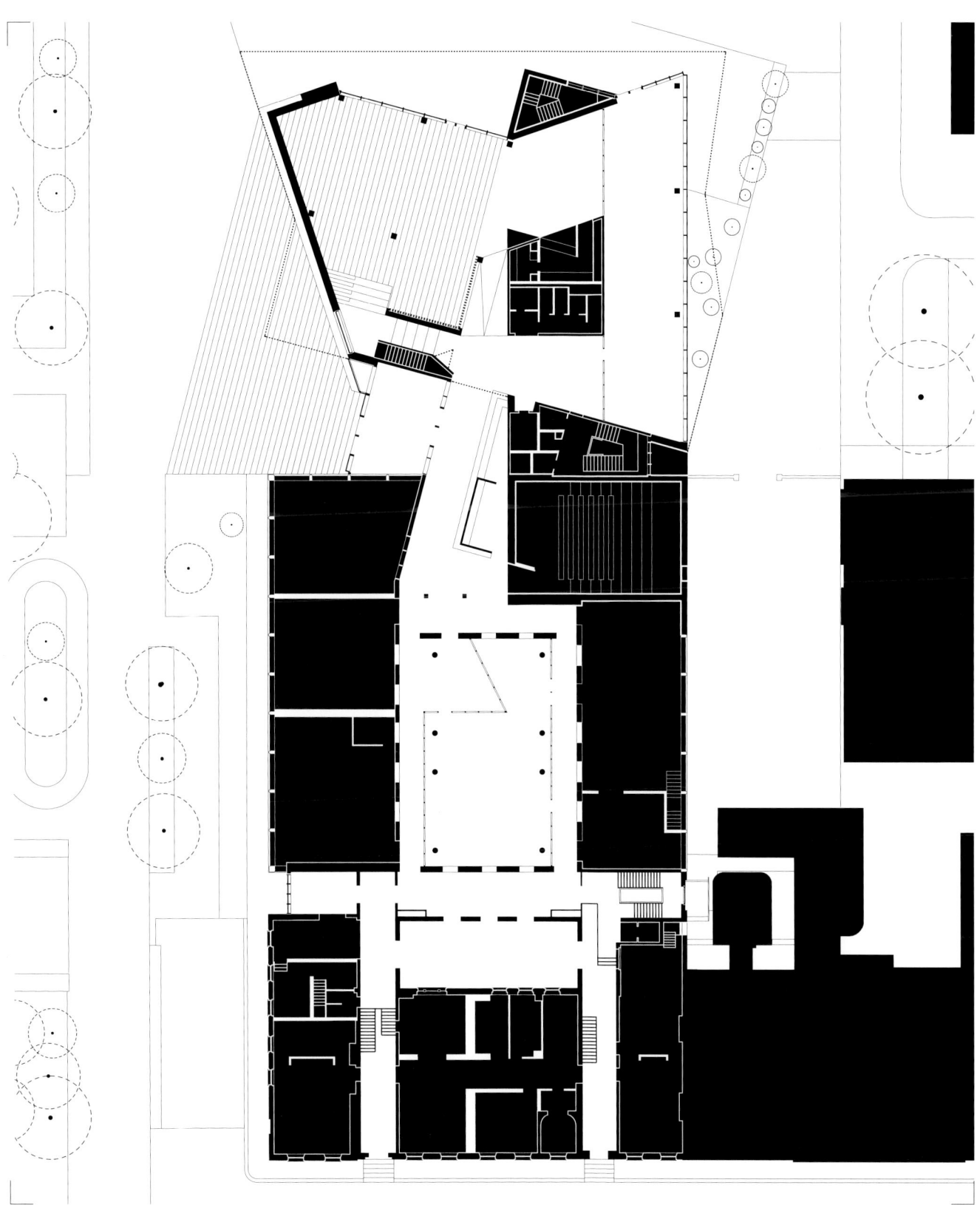

Intentions and Extensions

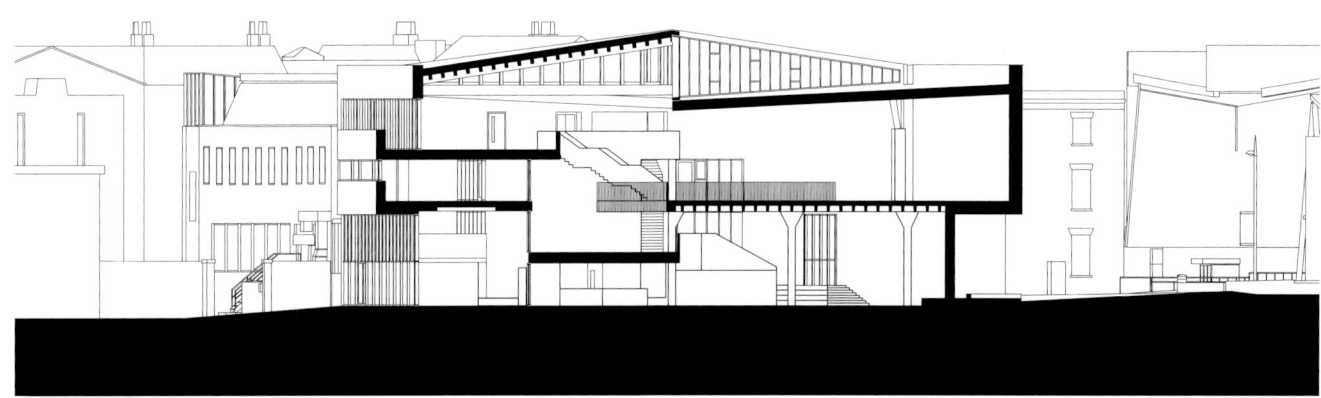

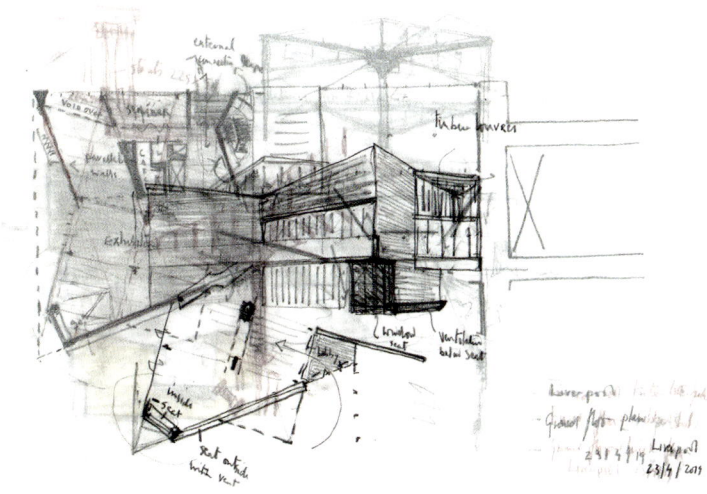

OPPOSITE TOP
Liverpool School of Architecture, Reilly, Budden, Marshall, perspective drawing, 1932.

OPPOSITE BOTTOM
Cross-section, studios over gathering hall.

TOP
First floor studios.

BOTTOM
Concept sketches.

Intentions and Extensions

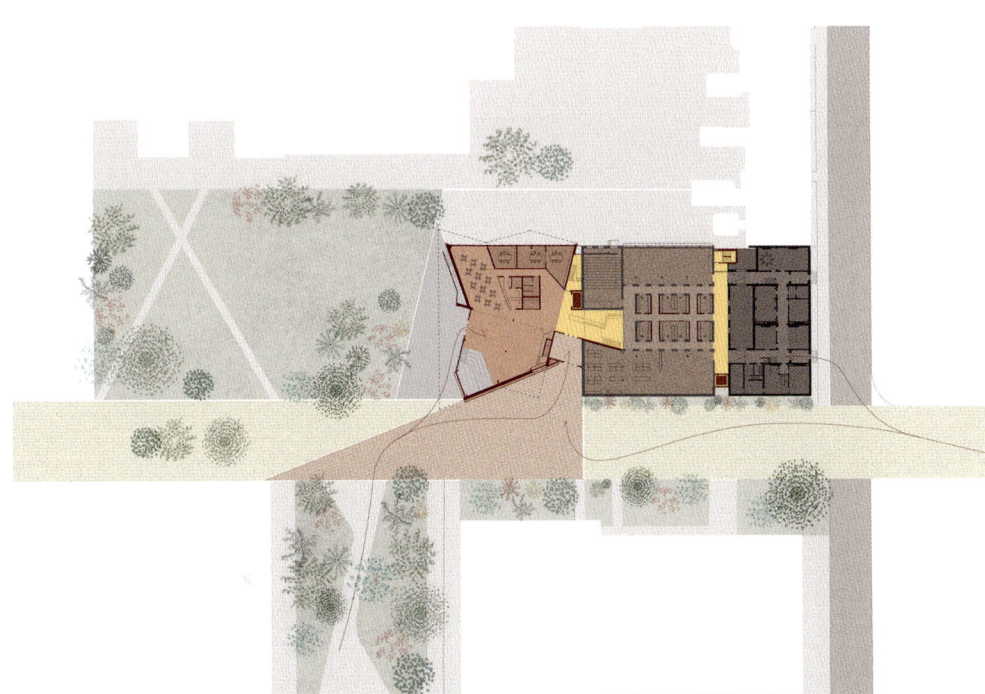

OPPOSITE
North-east corner view.

TOP
North elevation.

BOTTOM
Site plan in context.

Intentions and Extensions

Collaboration

Over the past decade we have embarked on an occasional series of collaborations with Joseph Walsh Studio, an internationally connected and exotically creative joinery practice with a committed team of master-craftsmen, all working out of a rural workshop in West Cork. Open-ended conversations about making and materials, public seminars and personal email exchanges have led to practical experiments in functional furniture and solid form. Typically, we would sketch up the outline of a design, the bones of an idea. Joseph would respond with his take on this, using it as a stimulus to produce a prototype mock-up leading us around to another way of thinking about the initial proposition. A special satisfaction is gained from seeing your sketchy ideas take shape in the hands of a perfectionist. Joseph seems to enjoy the temporary restriction that our architectural judgement places on his increasingly untrammelled freedom with wood bending in new forms. Both sides seem to recognise the mutual benefit derived from such an exercise, conducted within the safety limits of only sympathetic interference, a non-competitive sort of interference coming from outside your own discipline but staying within the common culture of studio practice, a break from the habitual autonomy of firmly established ways of working.

+ Vessel

The early work on what was later to be titled *Vessel*, for its installation at the Venice Biennale 2012, began out of conversations about roadside shrines, ageless places with a mysterious atmosphere, like the stone-lined tunnel space of St Brigid's Well near Liscannor in County Clare. *Rock of ages, cleft for me, let me hide myself in thee*. Memories of such places led us to a series of speculative studies in solid form and hollowed-out space. We made models in brown and white card to explore the effects of zenithal light, looking for ways of shaping space to encourage the descent of daylight down through a funnelled shaft to shine into a twisted passage below. Joseph was interested by our notebook sketches for one of these grotto-like but function-free forms. He didn't question the purpose of the project; he simply suggested that he might make a scale model in his workshop. When we saw the prototype taking shape, building up slowly in stacked layers of oak, we decided to add a little gold leaf to enhance the mysterious effects of illumination as it reflected in the folds and recesses, between the solids and cavities of the form.

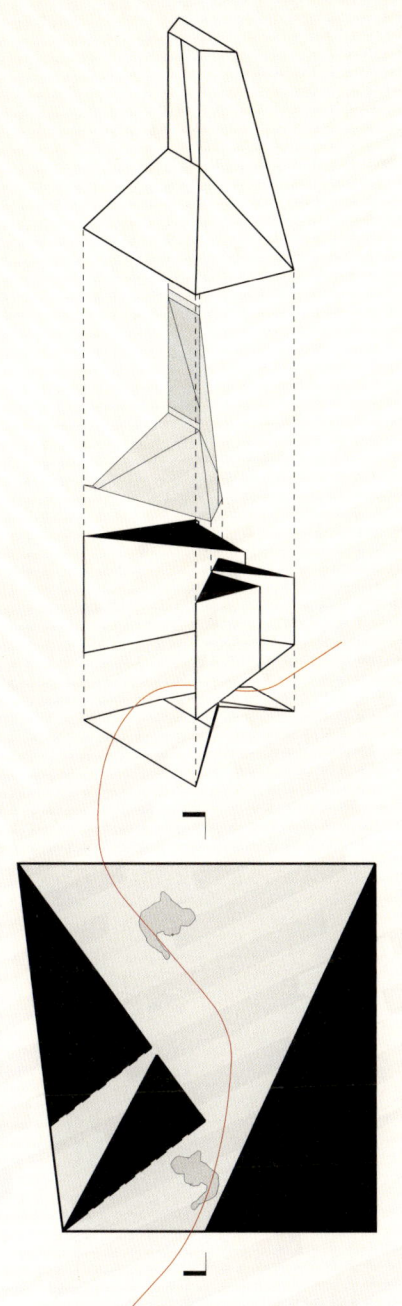

FRONTISPIECE
Vessel funnel, Venice Biennale 2012.

OPPOSITE
Brick and timber details at the Biennale 2012.

LEFT
Exploded axonometric, spatial concepts explained.

RIGHT FROM TOP
Oak and gold leaf;
Hollowed-out space.

ABOVE
Writing desk, flap down.

OPPOSITE
Furniture studies, sketches.

+ Falling Dansu

Another, this time more practical, collaboration with Joseph Walsh Studio was to work together on the detailed design of a contemporary bureau, a conveniently compact station for homework. We had been talking about falling tables, space-saving contraptions once commonly found in Irish traditional country furniture. Falling tables were made to fold up against a wall and, sometimes, in their closed position, they could double function as a window shutter. At the same time, following recent visits to Japan, we had been reading about traditional crafted objects of cabinetry known as *dansu*. These multicompartmental and portable medicine chests were carried about on the backs of travelling apothecaries during the Edo period. With such elegant exemplars in mind, we set out to develop a new series of functional furniture, the prototype for which we called *Falling Dansu*. It was made in ash ply, a plain wall-mounted box with moving parts inside, sliding shelves and secret drawers for personal papers, all of life's clutter kept hidden behind a carefully balanced leather-lined flap that could be tilted down easily to act as a writing desk and closed up quickly when not in use.

+ Unfinished Museum

This early version of the V&A East had to be set aside after two years' work because of client changes to the scale of the building and following fundamental developments in the museum concept, developments beyond the intended scope of the original competition brief. But still somehow, willing as ever to adventure out on a new excursion, welcoming the chance to begin again with a fresh start, this time with the opportunity for post-competition dialogue and more meaningful contact with the museum curators, we were left with an internal hankering for the volumetric composition of the superseded idea.

Projects have to stop when they're stopped—this is a practical matter, of course—but thoughts can't help but continue, lingering or, so to speak, turning over in the mind. Discussion with Joseph on how to handle the pain of this surplus-to-requirements situation suggested an interesting possibility. He wanted to try something different with stone, to develop a new material expertise in his workshop. We wanted to whittle the unsettled form of the initial idea down to its essence, to fix it in our life history. And so, we agreed to work together on *Unfinished Museum*, a semi-sculptural work, unfettered from its functional origins as a working piece of architecture.

Unfinished Museum was slowly hewn by hand out of a single block of Italian alabaster, weighing in at 350kg. Elements of the original design were edited out to open up the form, with other aspects gradually adapted to suit the structural capacity of the stone. Leading edges were chiselled away to meet at a sharp arris, giving a light-translucent solidity to this hefty exercise in spatial subtraction.

CLOCKWISE FROM LEFT
Stone carving at Joseph Walsh Studio; Alabaster, single block carved by hand.

OPPOSITE CLOCKWISE FROM TOP LEFT
Unfinished Museum, alabaster on oak plinth; V&A East, Olympicopolis, early version, developed design; Cross-sections.

The V&A East was one of the crucial components of our original *Olympicopolis* competition-winning design, the initial outline scheme that preceded the eventual as-built East Bank. That first design for the V&A had been inspired by our discovery of one particularly mysterious object among the myriad in the museum's extensive Japanese collection, a tiny inlaid lacquered box, an incense-smelling guessing game from the time of the Edo court. We interpreted the open drawers of this multilevel box as a spatial analogy for the invitational proposition of a contemporary open-access museum. We saw our project, not primarily as a set of cantilevered galleries, but as pockets of public-facing space, volumes hollowed out from deep inside the centre of the structure, with the inner workings of the museum revealed to its urban setting.

116   More Space for Architecture

Collaboration

+ Alternative Histories

FROM LEFT
Zaha Hadid, perspective studies, 1986; Model undercroft.

OPPOSITE CLOCKWISE FROM TOP
Sketches; Model; St Brigid's Well, Liscannor, County Clare, Ireland.

Alternative Histories was an altogether different kind of collaboration. It is said that every new artwork has at least two authors and at least one of those authors is dead. We were allocated a single page of pencil sketches drawn in the 1980s by Zaha Hadid, exploratory studies for an unbuilt office project. It was explained that this drawing, carefully selected by the curator who had spent "these past days spelunking the Drawing Matter archives in search of a drawing that might fit you", was now given over to us, ours to be freely assimilated and freshly interpreted for the Dublin leg of the *Alternative Histories* travelling exhibition. Each invited architect was asked to adopt the drawing that had been assigned to them, to "further the thoughts contained within", to seek their own way out from the cave of another's beginnings. The simple requirement was to make a new model for exhibition in response to the original drawing. We were more than happy to play along with the lively volumes indicated in these lovely sketches.

Around the time that she might well have been sketching out this super-skinny scheme, Zaha came to Dublin to lecture at the National Gallery. She showed her entry for Taoiseach's House competition, with its dynamic plan breaking out of the walled garden in the Phoenix Park. She explained her breakthrough beam-based project for the Hong Kong Peak and many other funny and brilliant works, possibly this unbuilt project too. At the end of her talk she agreed to take questions from the floor. An unidentified voice from the back of the hall asked whether her real ambition might not have been to build in outer space, given all those gravity-defying cantilevers and distorted perspectives. Zaha looked disgusted, shot the questioner a withering look and, with a sighing growl, replied with a room-resounding *No!*—how could anyone think she would be interested in floating around aimlessly in outer space? She wanted to work on real buildings on real sites, down here on the ground—*and anyway, it's not about those perspectives—don't you know that architecture begins with the plan?*

Since the colliding train carriages of her space-collapsing Constructivist diploma show at the Architectural Association in London, we'd been impressed by the linear geometry and pulled-apart plans of Zaha's planetary universe. Our subsequent enjoyment of the actual built work has been limited—moving moments in the MAXXI, the sinuous volume of the swimming pool in Stratford, and especially the disjointed elegance of the fire station at Vitra, which we saw when it was new.

We decided to start with the spatial proposition and to treat it at the scale of a house, rather than an institution. Working outwards from within the form, we reversed the stacking, introduced a welcoming stair and imagined an out-of-the-

picture-frame focal point for the dug-in building to aim itself towards, to ground the elements of the composition in a useful balance.

We began with the idea of an end-of-terrace plan, just as outlined in the initial sketches, but soon it became a solid-cast volume opened out, reaching to connect to some distant lines of view. The open space would be approached by a divided route through a convoluted base and up a winding stair. We cast the model in plaster to give this small object a bit of weight in the world.

Ideas in Things

One starting point is a belief in the physicality of architecture as its primary mode of communication. Buildings can be understood as physical evidence of human intelligence, speaking to us across time. They convey ideas through their concrete presence. A good building distils complex factors and forces them into a single comprehensible 'thing'. The fact that this thing might change its meaning over time doesn't take from this reality. William Carlos Williams, in his poem "Paterson", repeats the ringing phrase *"no ideas but in things"*. *Things* is a versatile word: it embraces useful objects, words, ideas, books, images. It encompasses experiences, personal belongings, undefined entities, landscapes and, yes, of course, the thing itself, the lasting value of a useful building.

> The Red Wheelbarrow
>
> so much depends
> upon
>
> a red wheel
> barrow
>
> glazed with
> rain
>
> beside the white
> chickens
>
> WILLIAM CARLOS WILLIAMS, THE RED WHEELBARROW

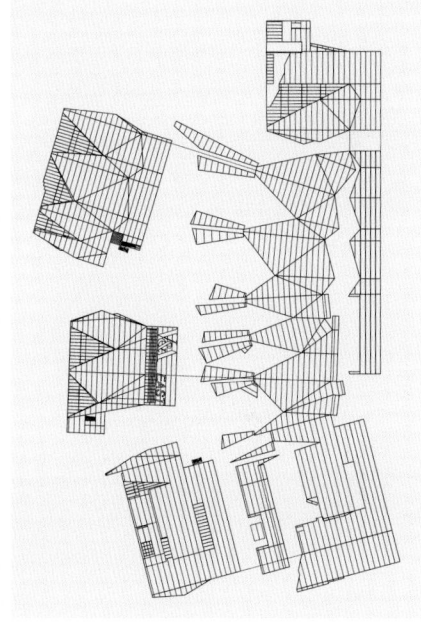

We want to make our buildings feel permanent, robust and ready for a long and useful life in the world. That's why we like to work with raw materials, the archaic stuff that weathers naturally and wears out slowly: brick, concrete and timber seem to offer some sort of aesthetic resistance—resilient as they are to time and season. But for the builder, this makes life a little more difficult—because the structure is the first thing to be made, outdoors in the wet and windy conditions of a building site, and these primary elements must be protected through all the messy stages of construction, eventually to emerge intact as a precious finish. The first thing made becomes the first thing visible, final finishes can't conspire to cover up defects in the early work. This is difficult to achieve in real life and we have seen well-made pieces of work suffer from the untimely drop of a scaffold pole or a blow from the end of a passing ladder. But the builder is a necessary part of the team, and must feel part of the family working together to make a good building. Architects must be ready to praise the work and learn to love the builder who is doing his best. Rilke, in his efforts to seek out space for poetry, told his patron Princess to "praise this world to the angel".

> ...So show him
> something simple which, formed over generations,
> lives as our own, near our hand and within our gaze.
> Tell him of Things. He will stand astonished; as you stood
> by the rope-makers in Rome or the potters along the Nile.
>
> RAINER MARIA RILKE, *Ninth Elegy*

OPPOSITE
V&A East, precast concrete sample; shadows and light.

ABOVE
V&A East; Unfolded facade, component construction study.

Ideas in Things

We could translate Rilke's lyrical advice to send praise to the angel, to much more practical, but no less poetic ends. Architects should speak directly to clients, contractors and tradesmen, talking simply about qualities near our hand: qualities that inhere in what Rilke liked to call "Things"—or in what we call buildings.

Architecture is a craft-based art. The architect's concept has to be carried across to live in the building itself, and this transference is realised through the active commitment of the contractor and the measured skill of manual work. Bricklayers, carpenters, shuttering contractors, site engineers and general foremen are the unsung actors that make actual architecture out of architects' intentions. These are the people worth talking to, worth taking into our confidence, and whose advice is worth listening to. Ideas are born in the mind, but architects' ideas live on in the practical poetical things we call buildings. Or, as Denys Lasdun is said to have said, "You can go and see it, and the building, if it has anything to say, will have to speak for itself."

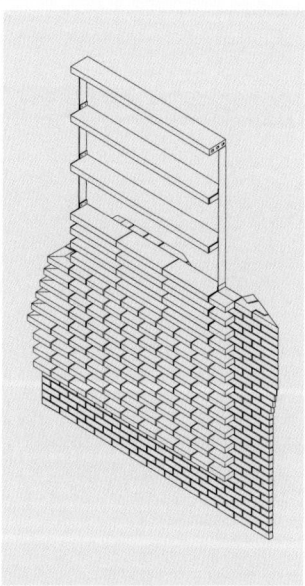

LEFT
Sadler's Wells Dance Theatre and Studios, brick specials, prototype.

MIDDLE
Sadler's Wells Dance Theatre and Studios, sample wall brickwork.

RIGHT
V&A East; construction site.

Professional training inclines our profession towards the view that craftsmanship is a thing of the past, and by this way of thinking, architectural design should avoid the demands of difficult construction and instead should provide for the norms of the industry. As if the building process should be, or could be, reduced to the assembly of standardised components. On the contrary, we have found that the whole construction team can rise to the satisfaction of seeing a difficult job done well. And we have had the good fortune to work with master-craftsmen and careful colleagues who attend to the discipline of their craft at every stage in the difficult journey from design to completion. Strangely enough, it seems that the more difficult the challenge, the better the chances of getting the work done well. This is one further reason for us to try to approach simplicity through complication; because if it's too easy to do, no one seems to think it's worth trying to do it well.

We practise our own craft through a studio-based way of working. First thoughts are sketched out in soft pencil, then quickly drawn up on computer and roughly modelled in cardboard. The process is repeated on a daily basis and designs are gradually developed with overlay drawings on A3 sheets of "*Skizzen*" paper. There is nothing novel in this routine; it's the technique we learned at Jim Stirling's office. It's the means by which fluency emerges, continuous in many respects with the methods of student project work. And, sometimes, on a good day, a mysterious jump in thinking happens when the work itself is in flow.

Constant practice in the studio helps to develop a surer sense of scale and some practical experience on site helps to keep the mind's eye and the hand's action

connected to each other. Working closely with trusted colleagues in the studio and cooperating with expert consultants is one of the tangible benefits of professional practice. Unlike in College life—where the hard question always seems to be *Why?*—in practice, more often the interesting question is *How?* This is the craftsman's question, the question of the role of process in the business of making. The search for an adequate answer can open up directions for collaborative investigation into the capacities of materials and methods of construction.

    This is <u>this</u>. This is not <u>that</u>.

Richard Serra, *Due Process*

LEFT
V&A East; steelwork manufacture.

RIGHT
V&A East; steelwork on site.

Ideas in Things

The technology of communication has changed completely in our generation. The principles of the tools of the trade have changed somewhat less. The raw materials of construction have changed very little. The really big change in building technology happened long ago, by the end of the nineteenth century—with the separation of structural frame from enclosing fabric. Walls these days are not monolithic, weight no longer requires massive thickness for its support, and buildings provide added protection from the weather in purpose-specific layers of construction. This is the breakthrough that, after countless centuries of masonry-based building, brought about the revolution in twentieth-century aesthetics of construction. Nowadays this news is no longer new.

ABOVE FROM LEFT
Limestone quarry, Carlow, stone for TU Dublin Academic Hub and Library; Limestone quarry, Budapest, stone for CEU, Central European University Budapest; Construction site.

OPPOSITE
V&A East precast concrete sample; lines and surface.

Timber, always a scarce resource, requiring management at source and maintenance in use, is still sawn in planks and joined in sections to allow for movement along and across the grain. And the technology of glass and steel is amazing in its complexity and refinement, but the difference is in degree, not in kind. Bricks have changed not at all—175,000 of them for the LSE Student Centre were individually made from clods of clay, hand thrown in wooden moulds, sprinkled with coloured sands and baked in the oven like loaves of bread. Construction sites are social settings, settings where the social art of architecture takes on its substance. And the quality of craftsmanship is always ready, like Rilke's angel, to be recognised with human respect shown at every stage from setting out to finishing off.

+ St Angela's College

CITY IN MINIATURE

St Angela's College is a long-established school on a steeply sloping mid-block site. The transition from feasibility to completion was a slow process lasting 16 years. Along the way, we worked with the school to make the case for its continued existence on this inner-city site, resisting the prevailing pressures for the relocation of city schools to the suburbs.

The project was developed out of a critical evaluation of the possibilities offered by the constraints of the context. The campus is designed like a hill-town, with lanes and courts connecting new and old together, like a topographical miniaturisation of Cork's urban conditions.

Despite the six-storey drop across the sloping site, and the crowded conditions of the context, new and refurbished spaces are naturally lit and ventilated. The convent orchard garden has become an extension of the arts teaching space. New interventions work their way down the hill, passing between historic buildings. A continuous external route negotiates the 18-metre drop in level, connecting orchard garden, courtyards, classrooms and playgrounds.

Four buildings were refurbished and two new buildings were added, one for sciences and one for arts. One challenge was how to incorporate a large sports hall on this confined hillside. A clear-span concrete structure was built on the lowest part of the site. Its roof, at street entry level, makes new ground for a ball court and sunny terrace with views over the city below. Another challenge was working with a standard school brief to a tight budget on such a complicated and non-standard site.

St Angela's College is an example of incremental urban development and resilient community life. The school is equipped to survive on its established site, enabled by the application of sustainable principles, to challenge the tendency towards urban sprawl and to continue its mission in the city.

FRONTISPIECE
Bridges and connections.

OPPOSITE
St Angela's College, entrance.

TOP
St Angela's College, existing site, aerial view.

BOTTOM
City view.

Ideas in Things

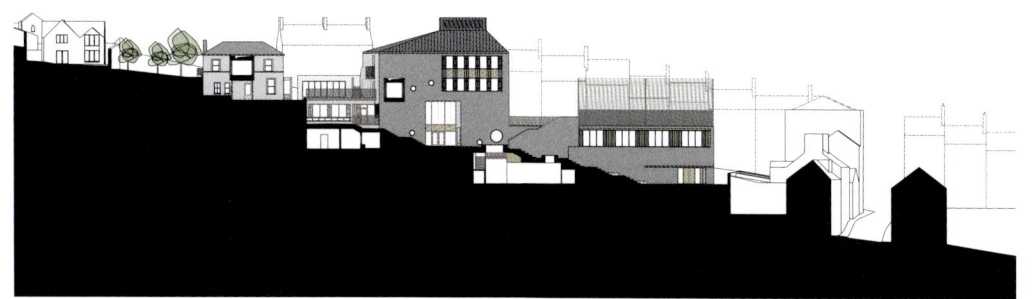

OPPOSITE
Urban context.

TOP
Stair window to cityscape.

BOTTOM
Long section.

Ideas in Things

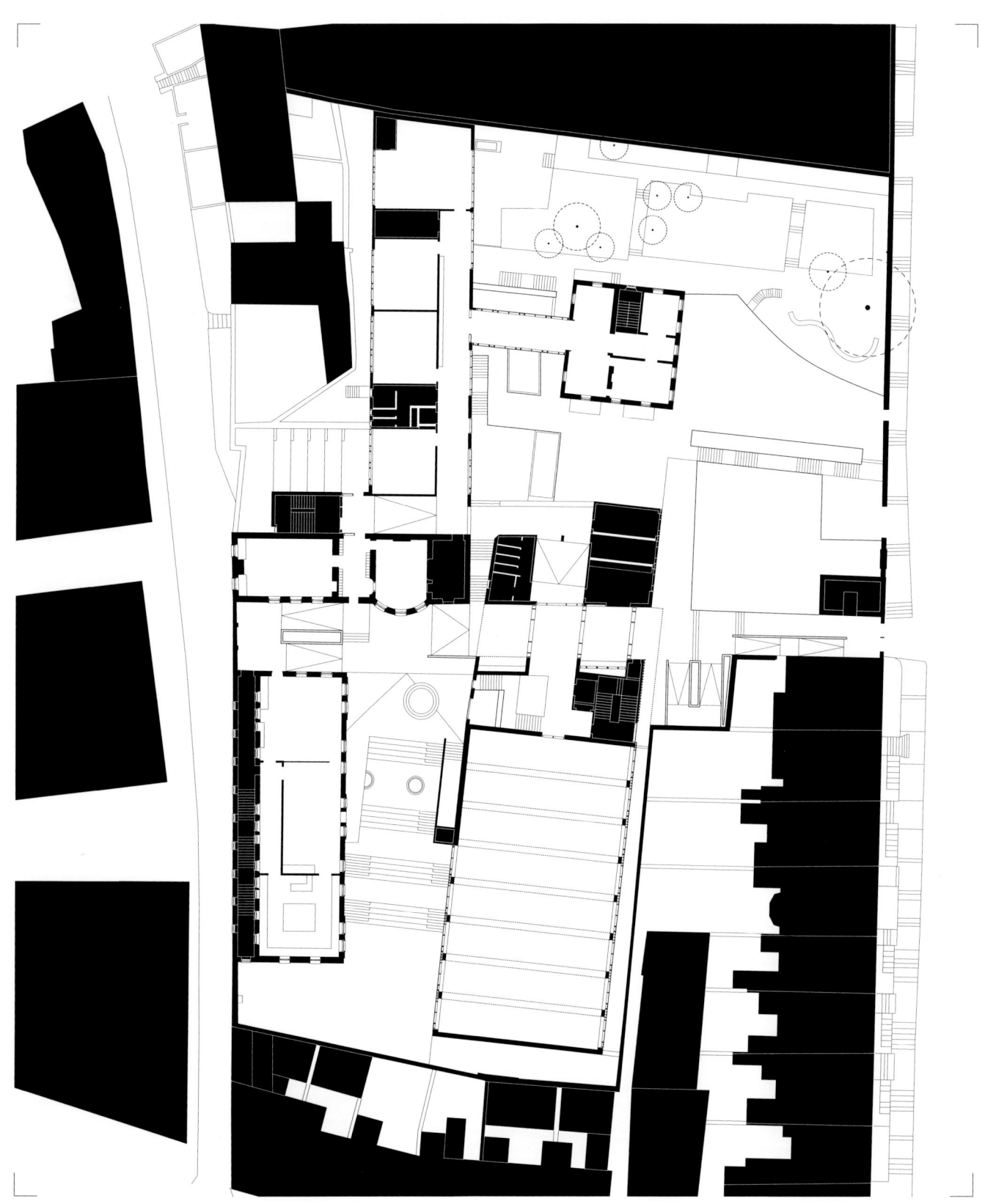

More Space for Architecture

OPPOSITE
Multi-level plan, scale 1:600.

RIGHT
Rooftop ball court.

Ideas in Things

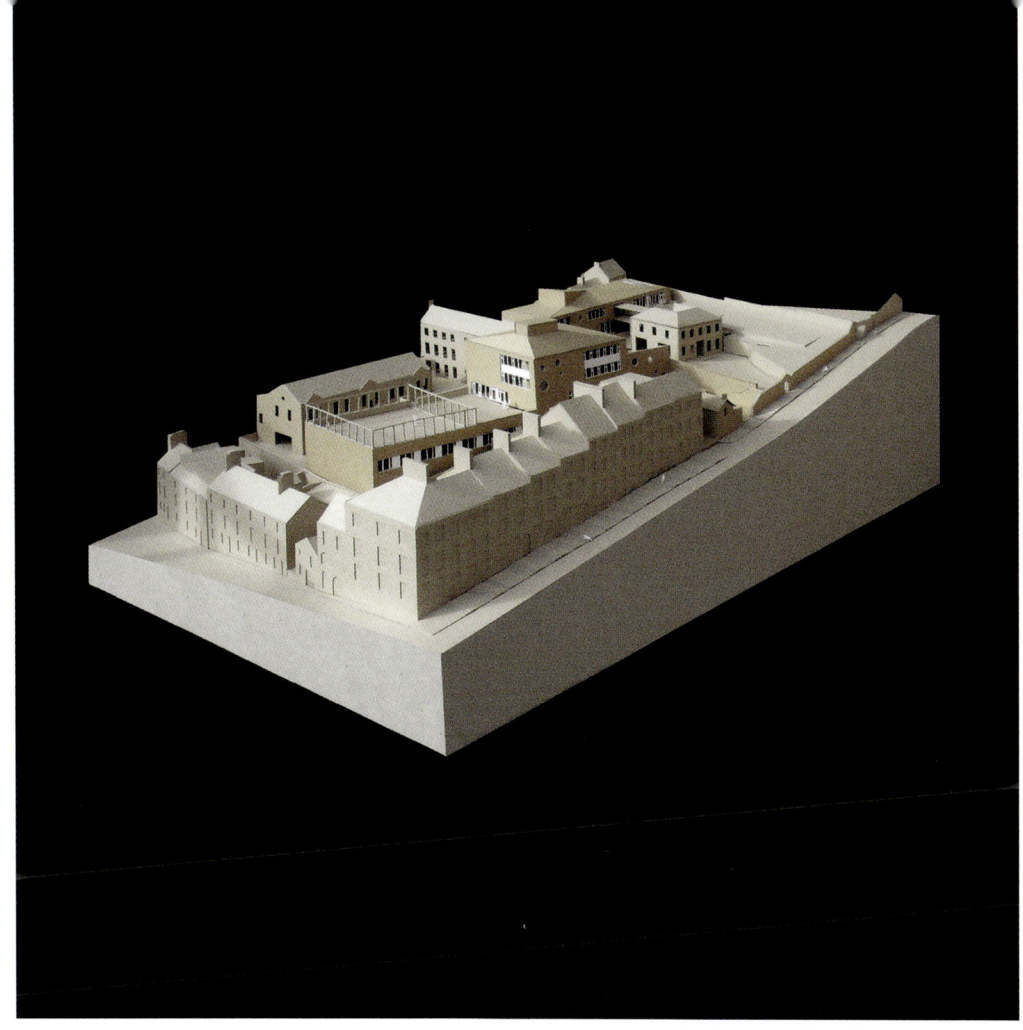

OPPOSITE
Courts and lanes.

TOP
Model in context.

BOTTOM
Cross-section, school hall and rooftop ball court.

Ideas in Things

CLOCKWISE FROM LEFT
Slate hung wall; School assembly; Sports hall.

OPPOSITE
Orchard garden.

OVERLEAF
City panorama, showing St Angela's College and Christian Brothers College.

The campus is designed like a hill-town, with lanes and courts connecting new and old together, like a topographical miniaturisation of Cork's urban conditions.

+ Christian Brothers College
STEPPING STONES

The new schoolhouse will add eight classrooms, a library, canteen and multipurpose hall to the existing campus, a boys' secondary school, with improved sports grounds and enhanced landscape connections between new and old. Patrick's Hill is known as Cork's steepest street and this dramatic situation has influenced the design of the school. Stepped terraces and gardens take advantage of the elevated setting, overlooking the city below.

The site, a long disused and overgrown quarry, with some mature trees, is directly across the street from our recently completed scheme for St Angela's College. The building will be built backed up against the cliff wall, facing out to the city. Each of its four levels opens out to newly established ground, making south-facing playgrounds, outdoor teaching spaces, and sheltered seating areas in between. The new structure links up with an adjacent existing building as it climbs the hill.

The school hall is on the lowest level, with the canteen above, then two floors of classrooms and a library sitting under the sawtooth roof, the angle of which follows the slope of the site. A simple arrangement of rooms and corridors extracts an element of energy from its interaction with a seemingly difficult site. Above the new schoolhouse, a playing pitch is integrated into the site contours, with brick retaining walls continuing the idea of the terraced landscape.

FRONTISPIECE
Schoolhouse entrance, upper level.

OPPOSITE TOP
View from Patrick's Hill.

OPPOSITE BOTTOM
Street elevation.

TOP
View from Patrick's Hill: Christian Brothers College to the left, St Angela's College to the right.

BOTTOM
Site plan with St Angela's College.

Ideas in Things 143

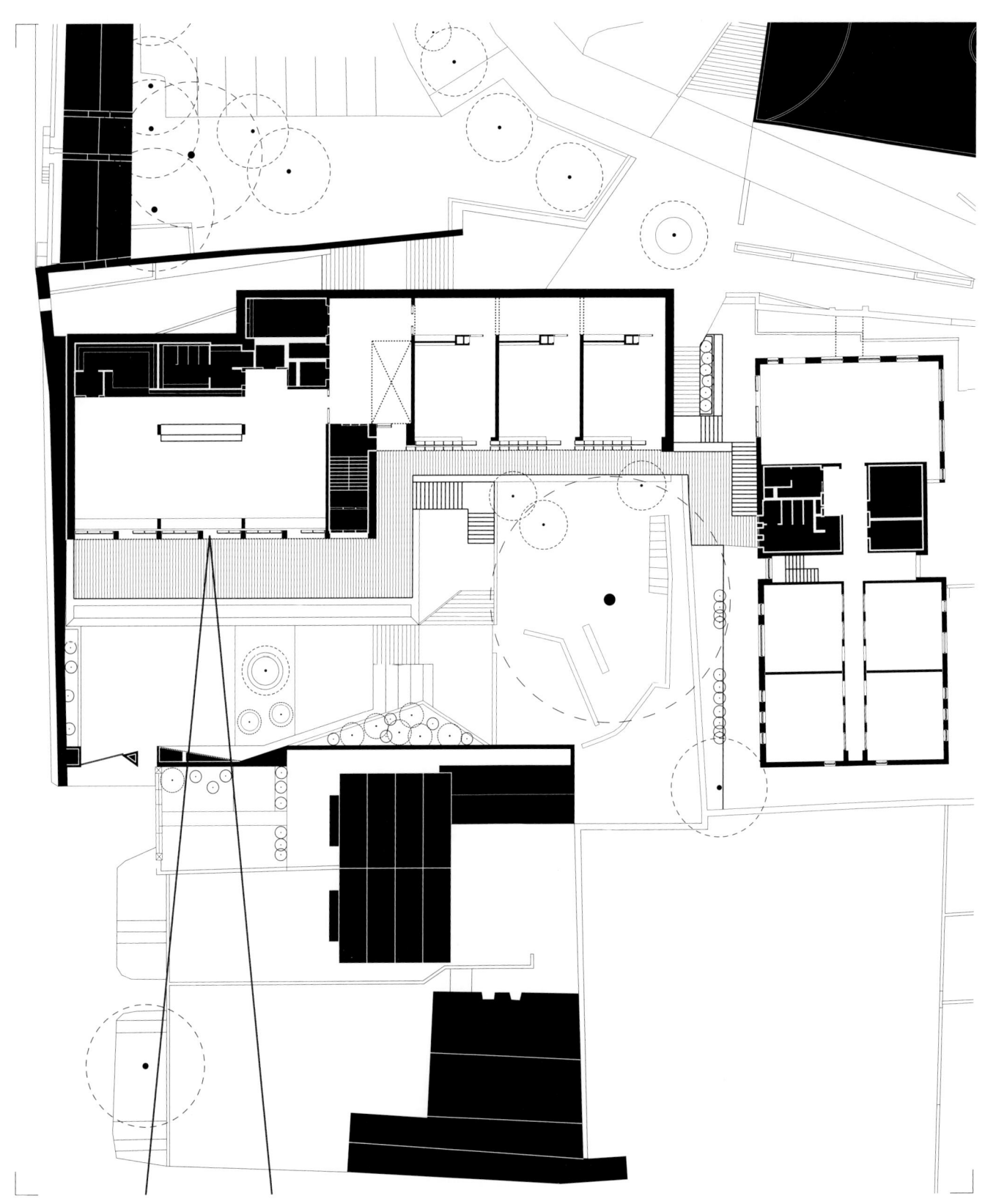

OPPOSITE
Plan, scale 1:450.

RIGHT
Entrance hall with stair lightwell.

Ideas in Things

+ Sandford Park Schoolhouse

PLAYSPACE

The new schoolhouse is part of a masterplan to guide future development at this long-established inner suburban Dublin school. It responds to a school-wide desire for space to encourage social life in between classes. At the heart of the building is a student forum, linking two floors and opening out to the playing fields. A covered porch makes a threshold at the end of the existing 'village street'. Along this street we have added brick carpets and concrete benches, new meeting points at each of the different teaching blocks. The landscaped forecourt includes an open canopy for gatherings, debates and performances.

On the park side, the schoolhouse completes a crescent set up by the old house, science block and canteen. Designed within a local conservation context, the new structure leans away to protect the privacy of neighbouring back gardens. The section opens up to bring in light and air. Ten classrooms overlook the playing fields. Corridors are wide, with seating areas for social interaction, lively spaces with high-level windows and timber trusses.

The structural timber frame rises out of a concrete base. Raw materials, concrete surfaces, timber trusswork with simple bolted connections, solid brick walls, strongly expressed vertical timbers and grey metal roofs were carefully detailed to be sympathetic to the arts-and-crafts character of the old school buildings. The intention was to find space for generosity within a standard brief, designing to a tight budget on a restricted site.

The next step is to design a theatre for performing arts, a further stage in the school masterplan.

FRONTISPIECE
School forum.

TOP
Typical classroom.

BOTTOM
Upper floor.

OPPOSITE
Plan, scale 1:450.

OVERLEAF
Schoolhouse in context.

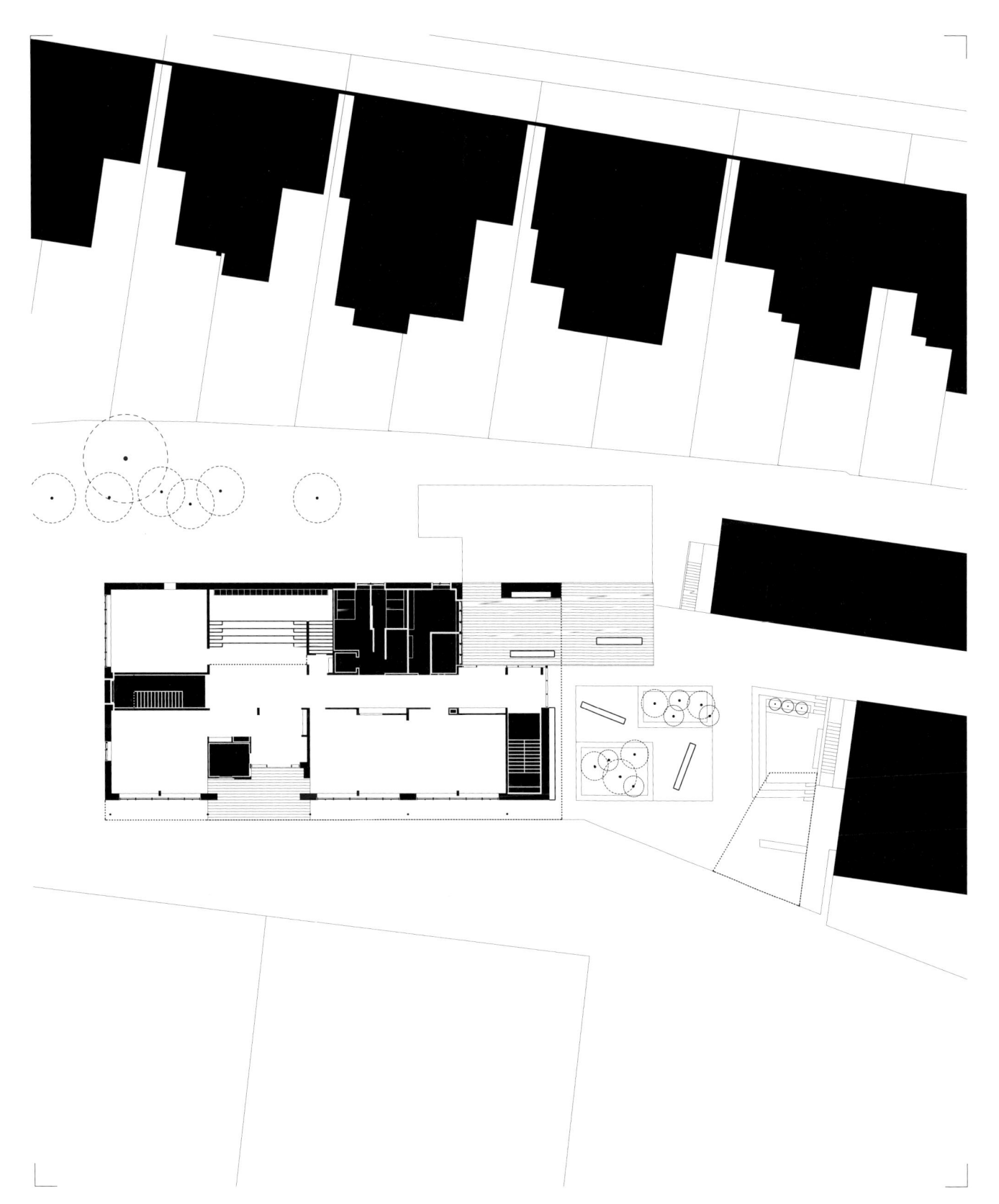

On the park side, the schoolhouse completes a crescent set up by the old house, science block and canteen. Designed within a local conservation context, the new structure leans away to protect the privacy of neighbouring back gardens. The section opens up to bring in light and air.

Ideas in Things

TOP
Timber details.

BOTTOM
East elevation.

OPPOSITE TOP
Campus masterplan.

OPPOSITE MIDDLE
East elevation of campus.

OPPOSITE BOTTOM
Cross-section, forum and classroom.

More Space for Architecture

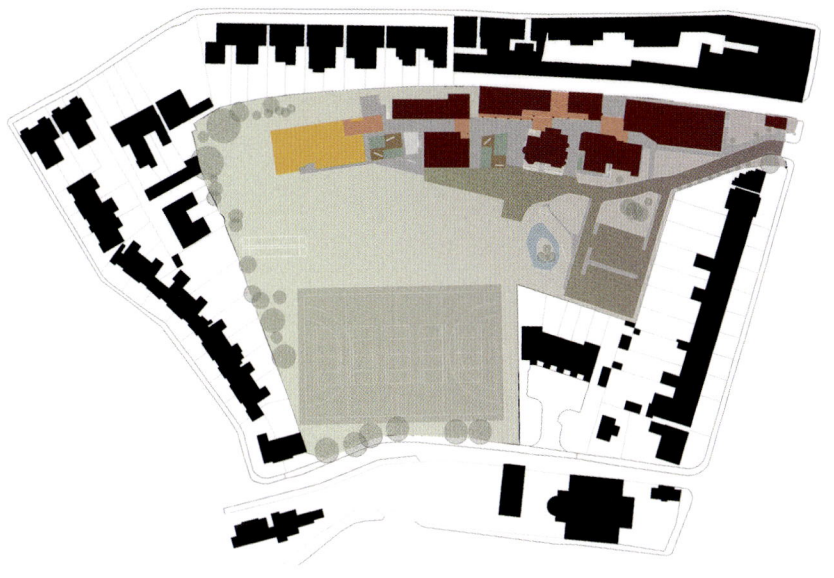

Ideas in Things

Watercolour Work

To me, painting trees during lockdown is relevant to our work. It's a way of thinking-while-looking about many things, things to do with: lightness and weight, texture and presence, scale and measure, structure and cladding, distance and nearness, shadow and light, colour and texture, weather and time.

A tree fits into its place; it shapes its surroundings. These factors affect how we think when it comes to making a building, how it might stand out and fit in. How it adjusts to its context, transforms it by its presence. How something just slightly askew charges the space in between. Five trees around a mossy stone make a space invaded by the presence of a wheelbarrow. Seven tall white trunks stand out in the sunlight, thin columns swaying against an ochre jumble of chimneys and the grey weight of the church that closes our vista.

Shadowy blue-green layers of rosemary, cut by the lines of twisted willows, their drooping masses of yellow-green leaves, hanging clumps quite separate from sinuous trunk and branches. Leaves on the acers turn from green to orange, articulating twigs and branches. Structure and form become one thing now. A vertically slatted fence marks the final layer of our garden enclosure, very small against the mass of the church beyond. The church stands at an angle, but its dome corrects the axis.

For years, I've painted mountain landscapes and distant islands as disembodied elements, floating mountains. I was interested in how distance, light and weather abstracted them into masses of colour and shade. I wanted to capture them as things, as supports for light and colour, faraway forms and free of detail. I wasn't interested in the detail; I was undistracted by bushes and rocky outcrops except as makers of shadow and depth. That's why I've avoided painting the foreground. I wasn't able to simplify it. My focus on detail got in the way; I'd get bogged down in accurate description.

Now, in the lockdown, I couldn't get to the mountains or islands, so I began painting what I could see in the garden. And it was all foreground. I started with individual trees, which are things, making it easier to understand what to do with them. And it was early spring, so branch structures were visible; small leaves and flower bracts were individuated elements, decorating branch ends or hanging delicately below. All parts clearly definable. The trees were chosen for structure, shape, bark and leaf colour. How they worked together to make spaces in the garden, to give shade or not.

Painting the fig tree across a number of days in early April made it easy to focus on structure and texture and the varied colour of its meandering branches. The thick verticals of the window mullions cut the image into strips, something to measure shapes against. When the leaves began to burst out it became a race against time to fix the bare structure. I moved on to paint a small group of trees, or one tree and its immediate background, then put them all together to describe the layers of the place. Describing the place, no longer the thing.

Which brings me back to the mountains and islands. Invited to exhibit my watercolour work at the Clifden Arts Festival, I wondered how to categorise the hundreds of small paintings I have made. I decided to show them in tightly clustered groups, arranged thematically as *Floating Mountains*, *Twiggy Branches*, etc. Each picture pinned to a white backdrop, each group protected by glass held in top and bottom rails but open at the side. They are not framed although, fixed like specimens under glass, they could escape out the sides.

I displayed these works in groups, as studies made in series, more process than product. They represent a continuing conversation with the landscape and with myself, done as a means of looking, of intensifying observation. They focus on form and light, and the relationships between things. They are partial views, attempts to pin down something of the physical and material quality of the landscape. They describe what is on my mind and in my eye. They relate to my work as an architect making form and space, working with the changing conditions of natural light.

OPPOSITE
Connemara sky.

OPPOSITE
Connemara mountains.

TOP AND BOTTOM
Twiggy branches.

OVERLEAF
Mountain view from the lookout, Caladh an Chnoic.

Watercolour Work

FROM TOP LEFT
Fig tree studies, 2020.

OPPOSITE
Acer, April 2020.

More Space for Architecture

OPPOSITE
Acer, October 2020.

FROM TOP RIGHT
Garden layers in lockdown.

Watercolour Work

Living in the City

Throughout the Covid-19 lockdown, in parallel with painting trees, I'd been working on competitions for social housing projects on special sites in Dublin, housing concepts grown out of looking at trees. The first competition was for three sites together, with no obvious connection between them other than their quintessential Dublin character, left-over corners of the city, awkward but full of intensity. One is a chess move away from Merrion Square, the second in the middle of the exhilarating nineteenth-century Guinness industrial city, the third on a busy suburban road, holding traces of earlier occupation. The second competition was for a street directly leading to Mountjoy Square, a visual extension of the plain-wall Georgian streetscape. We were asked to think about how to make each place part of its context, how the architecture of housing might reinforce the neighbourhood. The process had some similarities to close-noticing the trees. In this case, it started far out with an overview of urban connections, relationships to the city at large,

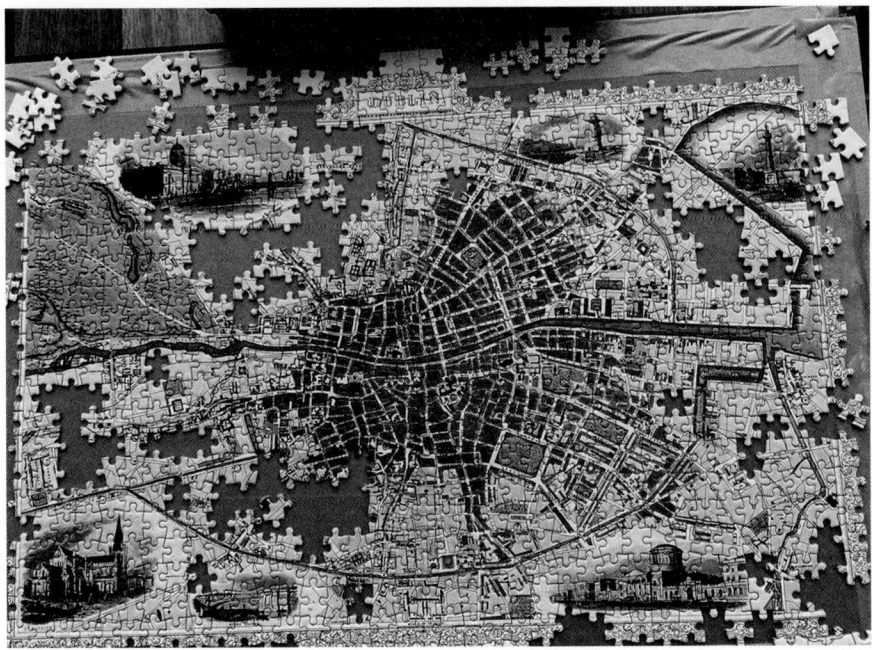

moving in to buildings and spaces on the site, and, finally, into rooms and hallways. Researching the history, walking the streets, observing the scale of each site from different viewpoints to develop a sense of urban form.

Housing has a universal character, designing environments at every scale; you might say, in a small way, that it's building the world. From the privacy of a bedroom window to the neighbourliness of a shared garden. Our work is strongly driven by use. The pattern of our design process involves functional analysis of activities, adjacency diagrams, environmental studies, study visits and time spent to understand the client ethos. The preparation for designing communal residential architecture is different. The practical purposes of the housing brief are well understood. The functional requirements may seem simple, yet housing is just as complex as designing a theatre.

OPPOSITE
Sunday's Well House living space.

LEFT
1000-piece jigsaw, Tallis map of Dublin, 1851.

Living in the City

LEFT
Timberyard Social Housing, city courtyard.

TOP RIGHT
Timberyard Social Housing watercolour studies.

BOTTOM RIGHT
Dublin Housing studies, 2021, deck access.

OPPOSITE
Dublin Housing studies, 2021, courtyard garden.

In the competition submissions we had described the sites as jigsaw pieces in the city plan. Months later, I received an unexpected present, a 1,000-piece jigsaw of the 1851 *Tallis Map of Dublin*. All three city sites are instantly recognisable in what was then a more compact city. Each of our sites is a piece of the jigsaw, joining other parts together in an effort to make sense of the overall. Your first encounter is with each piece as an autonomous thing, isolated, its orientation uncertain. Then, when it falls into place, it's no longer a separate thing, its individuality surrendered to the task of connecting. Making things fall into place is a big part of what we do. You mustn't force a piece to fit where it doesn't want to go; you must work with the logic of the whole.

The tree-watching and the jigsaw making are not idle distractions from the task at hand—they help to open doors to perception, to recognise layers of complexity, to examine the grain. They nurture our awareness of the architecture of the city. We have argued that designing adequate, ordinary residential neighbourhoods

is making the world or, to express it more modestly, shaping the city. We want to enhance the spatial experience from city street to private threshold, from civic space to communal garden, from shared deck to planted balcony, a secure and personal realm, a social world shared with fellow citizens.

Dublin was traditionally a city of houses, with buildings ranging in scale from one to four storeys. There's a lot of sky in the Dublin street. The big Georgian houses have taken on new uses, most of them now in multiple occupation. They were the starting point for our four- to six-storey Timberyard housing, completed ten years ago. But now we need to go up again in scale, to stop the city spreading further beyond its boundaries. The question now is how to build liveable neighbourhoods, with street continuity provided by buildings of six to ten storeys, and with the punctuation of taller structures where there is room for those points to stand in space.

OPPOSITE
Housing studies.

LEFT
Timberyard Social Housing, city landscape.

Living in the City

+ Sunday's Well Houses

HILL TOWN

Two houses are located on a gap site sloping steeply from Sunday's Well down to the marshland of the River Lee. The design was developed from a variety of contrasting conditions, starting from the tight pattern of the city at street level, through to the discovery of hidden views over the Lee Valley. This project is in conversation with its context and there is a parallel conversation going on between two houses, between two generations of the same family. Living spaces are slipped in between sleeping levels, with rooms opening sideways to the surrounding landscape.

One house responds to the more typical street condition, creating a bookend to the existing terrace of houses. Small bridged courtyards, lightwells and screens provide privacy, light and air, characteristic of the urban typology of the neighbouring houses. The south-facing living space with its sheltered terrace looks over the city to the distant hills beyond.

The other house relates to a number of nearby villas, individual houses standing out like wandering rocks, glacial erratics stranded in the valley landscape. This four-storey tower house is accessed at second floor level, by crossing a bridge onto the entrance terrace. The upper bedroom looks up the valley to the west. Living and kitchen areas on the middle floors open out to wide views of the city and its monuments. Ground floor bedrooms are screened by a canopy of trees. Steps and terraces connect with the gardens below. A stepped path through connected lawns leads to a sequence of terraced gardens, from expansive vistas to private hideaways.

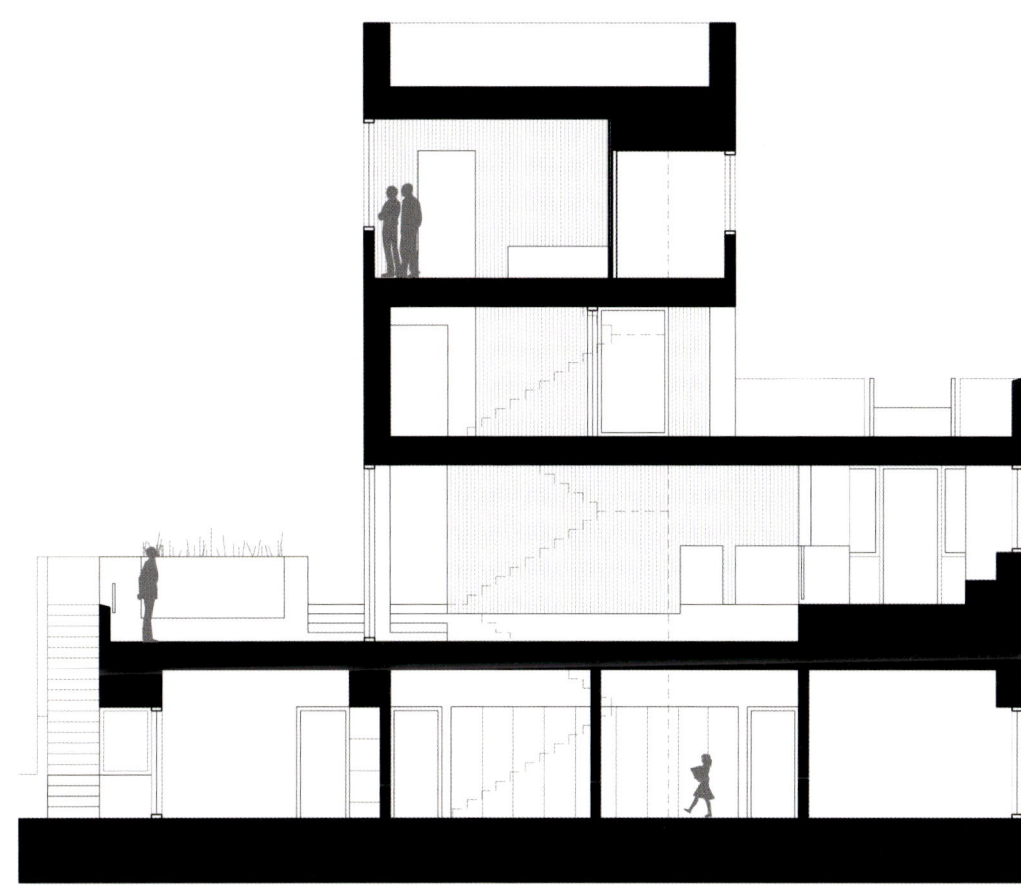

FRONTISPIECE
Terraced garden.

OPPOSITE
View to university.

TOP
Cross-section, living in middle floors, sleeping above and below.

BOTTOM
Site section.

Living in the City

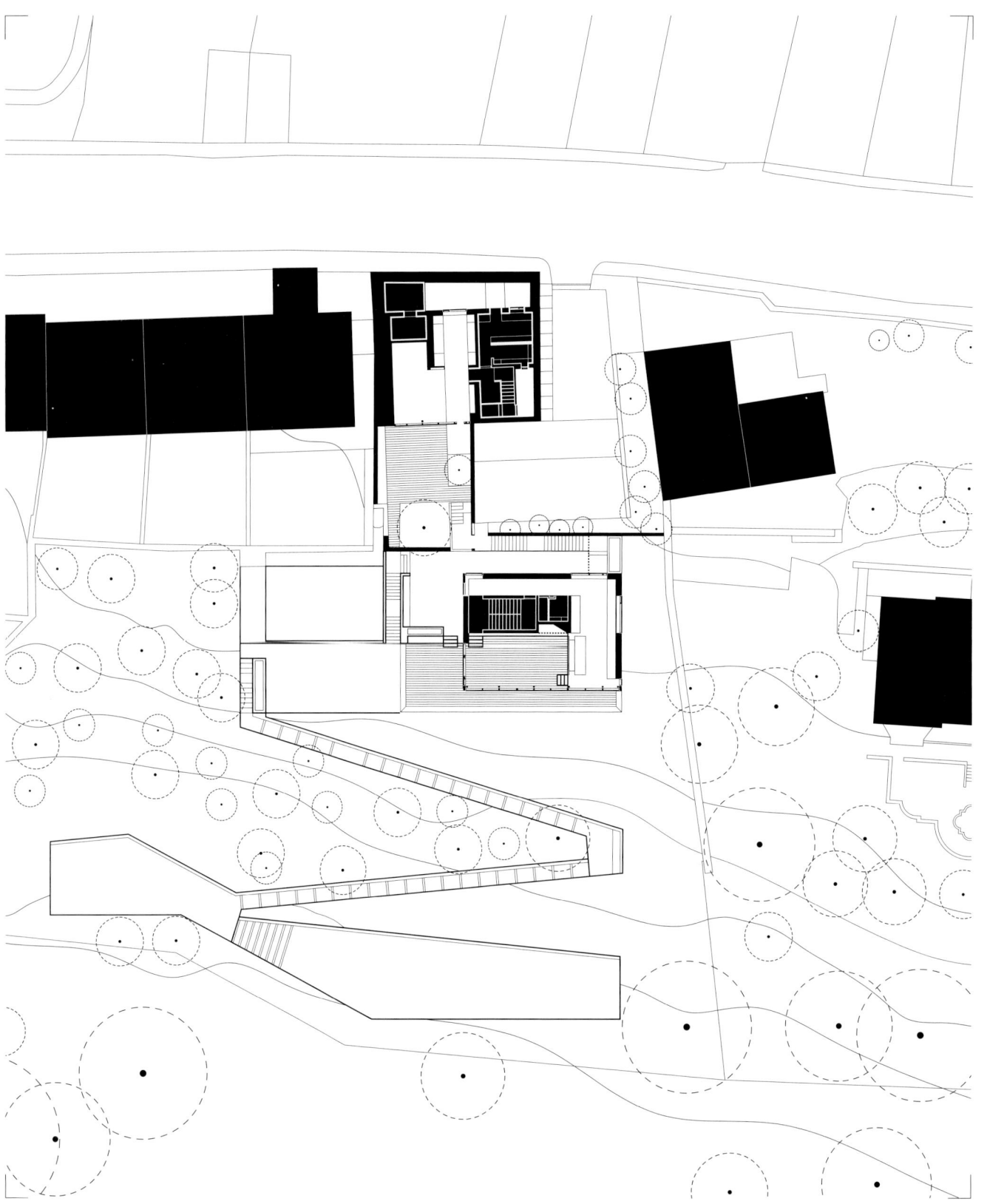

OPPOSITE
Plan, scale 1:450.

ABOVE
Kitchen.

OVERLEAF
Terraced hillside.

Living in the City

This project is in conversation with its context and there is a parallel conversation going on between two houses, between two generations of the same family. Living spaces are slipped in between sleeping levels, with rooms opening sideways to the surrounding landscape.

+ Clonliffe Apartments
SUBTRACTION AND ADDITION

The given masterplan indicated a wedge-shaped tower, intended as a landmark element, standing within the redeveloped density and retained parkland setting of the former Seminary complex at Clonliffe. We reconfigured the plan as a fan-shape to create dual-aspect apartments with open views to the park. The design was developed through a process of "subtraction and addition", with voids subtracted from the block to bring daylight to the circulation core. Roof terraces punctuate the vertical arrangement. There is a public cafe at the prominent corner of the ground floor plan. Deep-recessed threshold spaces define in-between territories for the residents' entrance hall.

The tower steps back to relate to the datum set by the parapet of the nineteenth-century Seminary. A second set-back helps to encircle the trees around the eighteenth-century Red House. It gets narrower as it rises, aligned on a visual axis with Jones's Road. The massing is broken down into a shifting arrangement of vertically composed four-storey volumes, rotated within a faceted form.

The profile of the building varies when viewed in the round. Set-backs and cut-outs mitigate the monolithic impact of a relatively tall building on the urban skyline.

The western facade is folded along its centre line in sympathetic response to the axis of symmetry of the Seminary elevation. The height of the tower, at 63 metres, is equal to twice the distance across the formal lawn. This sets up a balanced equilibrium between the linear elevation of the protected structure and the focal point of the tower.

FRONTISPIECE
Approach from the city.

LEFT
View across the park.

OPPOSITE TOP LEFT
Upper floor plan, with daylight cuts to circulation core.

OPPOSITE BOTTOM LEFT
Concept sketch.

OPPOSITE TOP RIGHT
View to old seminary.

OPPOSITE BOTTOM RIGHT
Cafe on the park.

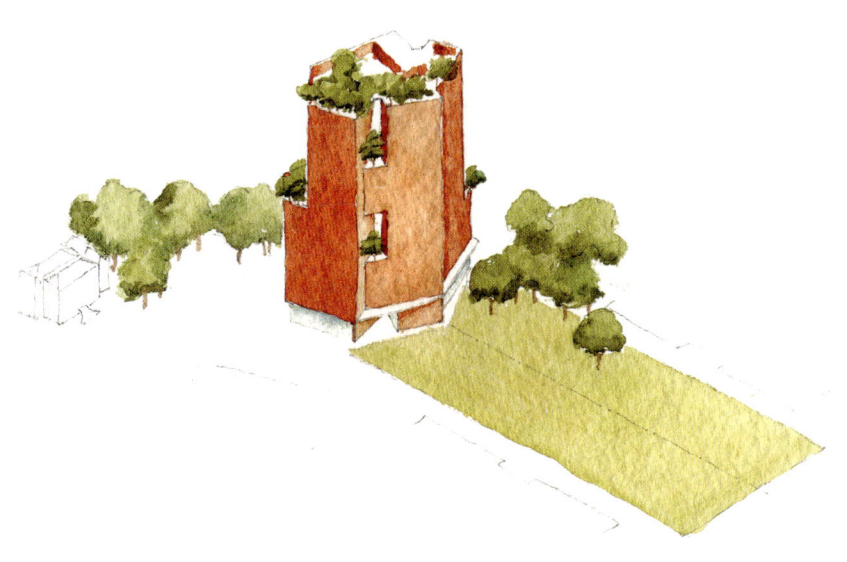

Living in the City 181

Folding Landscape

New buildings can contain memories and anticipation, memories of things that haven't happened yet. We try to build a sense of anticipation into circulation spaces as they weave through our buildings, by calling on our own distilled, blended and sometimes skewed memories of places we've visited, films we've seen, books we've read. Words themselves help us identify the combination of materials, shape, connectedness. We hone in on the spatial experience and try to assess specific aspects of character and effect. Repeated revisiting confirms whether the primary response is to the actual place, not only to lunch on a particular day, or the light of a beautiful evening. Place triggers memories, like retracing steps in Rome, but it's more accurate to speak of the physical experience of spaces. Eudora Welty explains it better.

> It is by the nature of itself that fiction is all bound up in the local. The internal reason for that is surely that feelings are bound up in place. The human mind is a mass of associations – associations more poetic than actual.
>
> EUDORA WELTY, PLACE IN FICTION

The novels of Willa Cather explore the physical characteristics of place, and how this place-memory affects people. At the outset of *Death Comes for the Archbishop*, a small group of cardinals and bishops are dining on a terrace high over Rome, taking in the evening sun. The titular archbishop is hoping to be appointed to New Mexico, where the church could spread its influence. The book sees him travelling by mule, or on foot, through the harsh landscapes of New Mexico. Cather captures, in beautiful passages of descriptive writing, vivid relationships between place, time and the living cultures of different peoples. The fact that the archbishop and his priest companion come from Europe means we are seeing New Mexico through their unfamiliar eyes. Their response to this new landscape is the context of the novel.

Our work in Connemara—in fact, our own work as a partnership—started with the 1977 Roundstone competition. We were living in London then, so couldn't visit the site—in those days you didn't so easily hop across the water—but we both remembered Roundstone from childhood holidays. We hadn't visited there together, but we shared some sense of the place, not necessarily accurate, yet each in accord with the other. Those seemed good conditions for work, to conjure up through conversation a collective of typical buildings from a hazily remembered version of the actual reality.

It was reading Aldo Rossi, learning about Terragni and the Italian Rationalists, that first got us interested in the topic of typology. And this study prompted further researches into the vernacular of the Irish landscape. Tracking down all those anonymous tower houses, barns and handball alleys—simple forms, stark in their relationship to the land, contaminated by lean-to additions, casual adjustments caused by need or climate—left us with a fascination for typical buildings just as they begin to deviate from type.

The Roundstone competition was for factories, workshops and houses on a seaside site, with a stone seawall elegantly curved, a granite pier overgrown with grass and the ruined tower of a Franciscan monastery. We arranged four buildings on

OPPOSITE
Folding Landscape/ East and West, Venice Biennale 2018.

ABOVE
Tim and Máiréad at Nimmo House with Sheila.

three sides of the tower to form a space open to the sea. Each building type had its own function-specific roof form: a terrace of vaulted houses, a row of pitched-roof workshops and factories with sawtooth northlights. The seawall was breached by an inlet with a pier on one side, for deliveries, and a beach, for leisure, on the other. We were interested in the switchback curve of the seawall, the rootedness of the monastery tower, seeking a typological clarity between contrasting structures. This early project's energy comes from the pull of orthogonal forms against that natural curve. It was driven by a sense of form in place.

The constructions that inspire us are not always made by people. We learn from the experience of the natural landscape. The gap behind a small cliff-face on Inis Meáin brought to mind the narrow alleys of some half-remembered city, with its so-to-speak facade, a vertical slab of limestone, separated from the ground by time

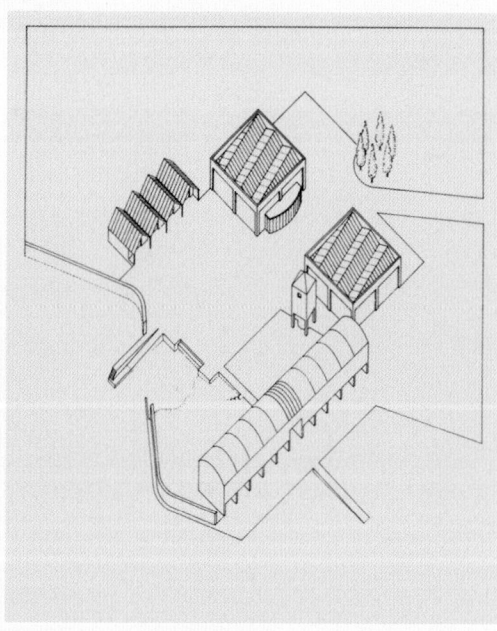

LEFT
Inis Meáin rock formation.

RIGHT
Roundstone factories, workshops and houses, O'Donnell+Tuomey competition design, 1977.

OPPOSITE LEFT
Tim Robinson, portrait by Mick O'Dea.

OPPOSITE RIGHT
Tim Robinson, drawing study for painting.

and weather, the space behind darkening as it narrows, all in the shadow of an enormous stone overhang. How to translate the lesson of this natural formation into the spatial configuration of any building we might make? We had visited that place many times before we began to notice this *rockopolis*. Our attention had been focused on the eighth-century chapel of *Lúb Cill Cheannanach*, its tiny walled enclosure roughly paved with disrupted layers of limestone gravestones. Maybe you only notice things when your mind is ready for them, when the need for a cliff-city is already there in your mind's eye. The weight of this edge-condition was reminiscent of the form of the Robinson Centre, a singular, one-material concrete shell, a jagged outcrop on its own small cliff.

We are used to making stories out of places, making new places within those stories. The best stories have a strong sense of place. Response to place is not a

Folding Landscape

singular one, never a simple one. There is more than geography to respond to. Adding any new building is a serious act. We would want to celebrate an existing quality, to bring out some essence, not only to add something new—as if we're trying to make the built object disappear in favour of the felt experience of being within it.

The half-landing of a stair might feel as if something has happened there: the participants have moved on, leaving something in the air. Or something is about to happen; it's not completely empty, maybe it's waiting. A shadow memory. An individual could be comfortable there, alone without emptiness. When Emmett Scanlon, in his recent podcast, asked me to respond to the question: *What Do Buildings Do All Day?* my first response was that buildings wait, and they remember. People can linger in the in-between spaces, waiting to be ready before entering, entering slowly perhaps. And the building waits too, for human activity, anticipates it, encourages the delayed response.

ABOVE
Cormorants.

Tim Robinson's empty house in Roundstone is waiting now. Waiting and remembering. The water that seeps from the sea up into the floors, and pours from the sky down into the ceilings, is abundant in its evidence of abandonment. But the objects they left behind challenge these signs of neglect. The mirrors, carefully placed, still reflect the sea and sky into the room, the fossils on the window sills continue to resonate. The artefacts themselves seem to question whether those old inhabitants are gone for good. Buildings hold sentiments, or perhaps our imaginations impose them. But these sentiments arise via powerful forces, subtly insinuated through structures and gradually instilled by sympathetic osmosis into us.

> Streets that follow like a tedious argument
> Of insidious intent…
>
> The yellow fog that rubs its back upon the window-panes
> …Licked its tongue into the corners of the evening
>
> TS Eliot, *The Love Song of J Alfred Prufrock*

By the time we started work on our project for Nimmo House, we knew it well. Layers of information, knowledge, impressions, had already accumulated in our minds. It's interesting to think how we come to understand a place and how that knowledge adjusts with each new revelation. In this case we knew the house, from outside only, as the home of Tim and Máiréad Robinson, with its odd sidestep away from other buildings at the end of the pier. It was, at one and the same time, the most visible and the most mysteriously reticent house in Roundstone.

Once, in the 90s, before we got to know him better, I had called at the downstairs door of the *Folding Landscapes* studio to ask Tim if he would talk to my students about Árainn. He politely refused, but then invited me in to see the map he was working on, spread out large on the studio table. I got an impression of an underworld warren, of low-ceilinged, multi-windowed rooms looking out to sea. Books, maps, stones, fossils and bones were scattered on shelves and window sills. The carpet was spongy with seawater and smelled of damp. I could see up the concrete stair to glimpse the garden and living quarters above. His later essay, "A House on a Small Cliff", a poetical text about space and place, brought us deep inside the upper rooms and the unfolding garden. He described a roof-lit house as it reflects moonlight and channels sea light through its spaces, multiplying reflections in its many artfully placed mirrors.

There are circular jumble-sale mirrors looking each way along this corridor; in fact the house has so many mirrors, glazed doors and windows that a diagram of how scraps of sky and garden are multiplied within it would look like that of an optical instrument.

TIM ROBINSON, *My Time in Space*

LEFT
Roundstone from the Robinson Centre with the Twelve Bens.

RIGHT
Tim Robinson, *My Time in Space*, 2001, Lilliput Press.

+ Robinson Centre, Roundstone

HOUSE ON A SMALL CLIFF

This study was commissioned by NUI Galway at the invitation of the benefactors of the site, Tim and Máiréad Robinson. Having participated in their Roundstone Conversations, having measured the house in careful detail with UCD Architecture students, having studied the planned village of Roundstone, having known the place since childhood holidays, having had ten years' engagement with the Connemara West community development in Letterfrack, having boated across Bertraghboy Bay, we slowly began to sketch out an architectural design.

The significance of the site begins with the sensitivity of the Connemara landscape. The building began as a storehouse for Nimmo's nineteenth-century pier-building campaign. Its industrial use continued as a knitting factory. It served as the centre of map-making activities and home-base for the intellectual research and work-life of the Robinsons. The question asked of us as architects was to propose a culturally driven design strategy for its continuation in creative work and discussion of ideas, to suggest future prospects for the Folding Landscapes site.

The refurbished house provides a cafe and meeting room to maintain the tradition of the Roundstone Conversations. A gathering hall for exhibition, performance and conference is housed under concrete mono-pitches, with clerestory roof-light to the gallery space. An upper loft space provides a lookout for sea-gazing visitors. A second building, located across Tim Robinson's numerical garden, holds private accommodation for artists' studios. The aim is to create a cluster of buildings within the sea-facing skyline of the surrounding context. A composition of clearly defined volumes, which merges with the undulating ground of the site.

>...there are moments in this room when time itself is perfectly content
>
>TIM ROBINSON, MY TIME IN SPACE

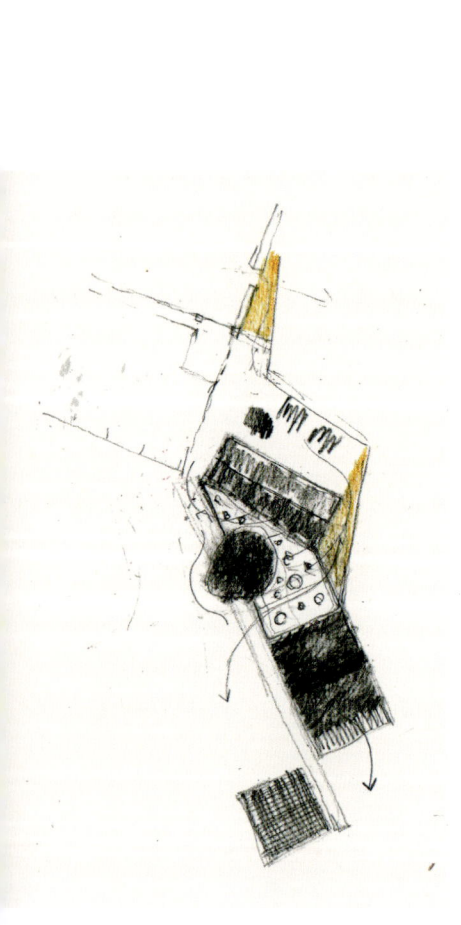

FRONTISPIECE
Roundstone Pier, Nimmo
House to the left.

CLOCKWISE FROM TOP
Nisyros obsidian stone;
Site walking sketchbook;
Concept sketch.

OPPOSITE
Plan, scale 1:450.

190   More Space for Architecture

192   More Space for Architecture

OPPOSITE TOP
Concrete model.

OPPOSITE BOTTOM
Cross-section.

TOP
Elevation to the sea.

BOTTOM
Nisyros pumice stone.

Folding Landscape

+ Folding Landscape/East and West
VENICE BIENNALE 2018

This installation in the Arsenale combined common aspects of two compatible projects. It played on similarity and difference, getting inside the ideas and outside the form of two quite different designs made for utterly different waterside locations and at wildly different scales —a current project in the West of Ireland and a recent competition finalist in China. At scale 1:2; a civic space, for public gatherings and studio retreat, sited at the end of a pier in Connemara. At scale 1:10; a city of opera, with interlocking foyers, theatres and roof-gardens, located at a bend in the river in Shanghai.

The visitor might have recognised the matching roofscape of both projects, their sawtooth skylines rising between the columns of the Corderie. A central stair led towards a south-facing window. Climbing up the sunlit passageway, between seemingly similar elements, a viewing point allowed you to look out through the old high window, then a second stair led you down again to divide your direction—eastward, to see into the Shanghai opera house section, or westward, to walk into the volume of the Roundstone gathering hall.

In one sense, independent of the actual exhibition contents, the spatial experience drew attention to the light from the window and watery reflections from the canal below.

The installation might also have been understood in a different sense, full-size at scale 1:1; a testament to our own experience of whitewashed monastery chapels in Greek mountain landscapes, where built ground is integrated with building form, where east meets west.

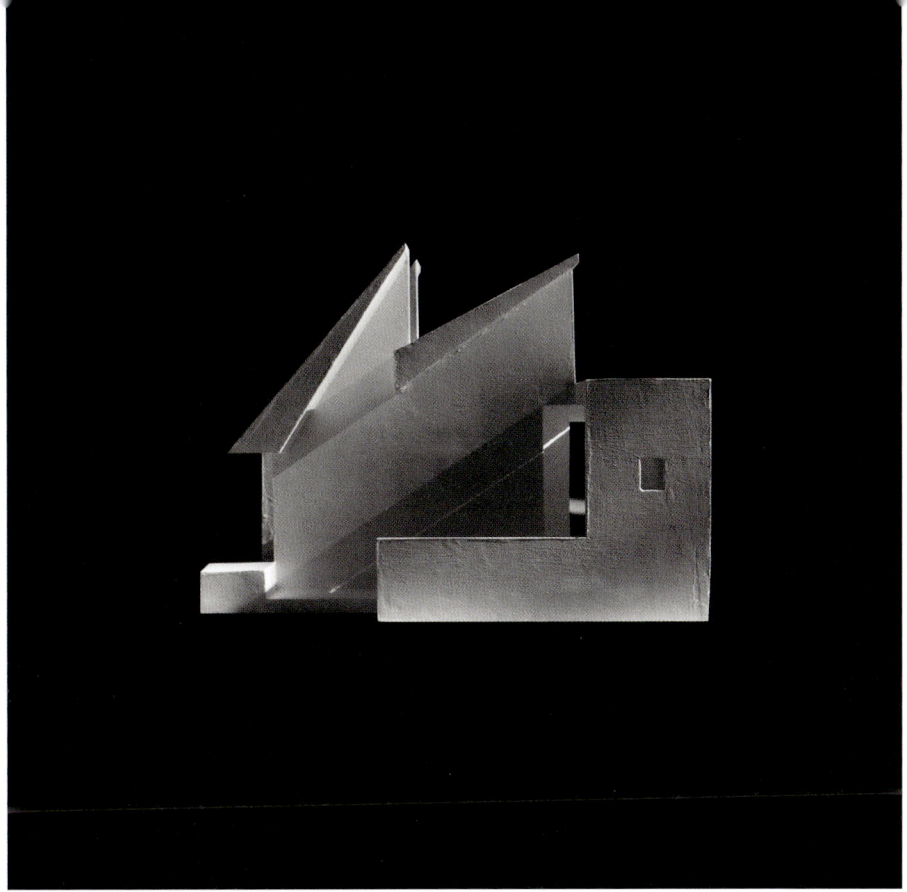

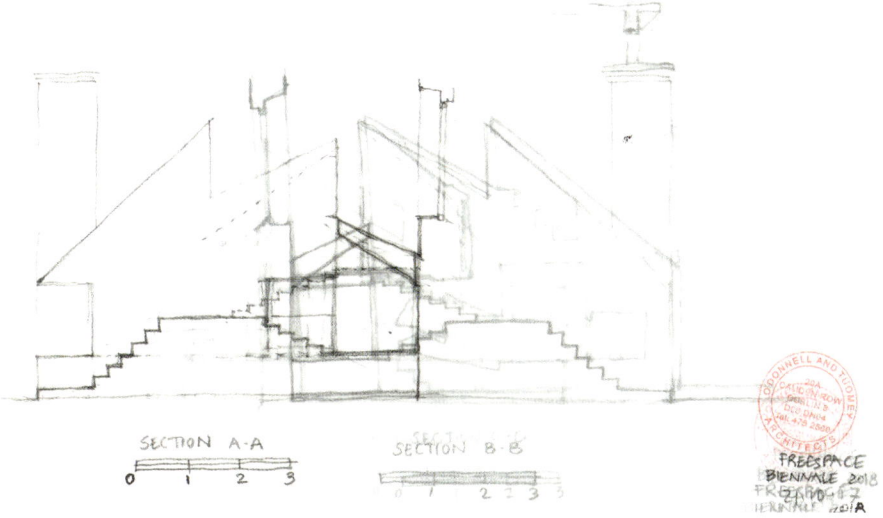

FRONTISPIECE
South light reflected from Fondamenta de la Tana.

OPPOSITE
Installation in the Corderie.

CLOCKWISE FROM TOP
Model, plastercast; Light from the window; Sketch sections overlaid.

Folding Landscape

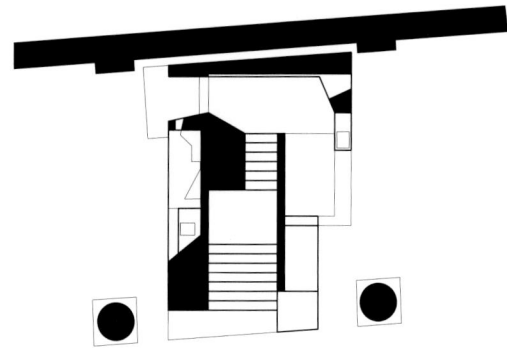

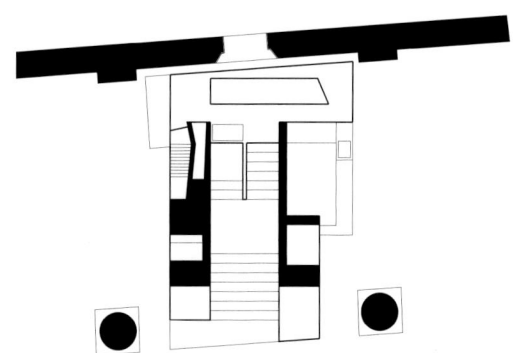

More Space for Architecture

OPPOSITE
Plans, scale 1:250.

TOP LEFT
Upstairs downstairs.

TOP RIGHT
Shanghai Grand Opera House section at scale 1:10.

BOTTOM
Drawings display wall.

Folding Landscape

Foyers—the sorts of spaces that occur in the in-between, between the open street and those indoor rooms where programmed activities predominate—continue to preoccupy our attention. These are the charged spaces that anticipate the play, that prepare us for the work, places of coming and going, accommodating stillness and solitary onlooking. Such spaces are associated with cultural buildings, but they can be found in buildings of any scale and type, outdoors and indoors, in schools, community centres, even private houses. In some ways they are dependent, therefore might be seen as secondary, their geometry not fixed, their boundaries deriving from the demands of functionally defined interiors. Yet these in-between zones are primary too. They are the spaces through which a building introduces itself; their function is to welcome, releasing us from a world over-focused on intensity of purpose. The key point is their in-betweenness: a loose fit between public and

private, between old and new, between inside and outside, a comfort in occupation. Understanding these spaces comes from reflection in experience, from noticing, from the noticing of noticing, from unconscious absorption and conscious recall of lessons learned at the appropriate time.

The guiding principle of Scharoun's design for the Berlin Philharmonie was 'Music in the Centre'. The entire building responds to the unusual form of the auditorium placed asymmetrically above the foyer. The dynamic of the foyer is generated directly by the pressure of the great raked room overhead. In that sense, it is all negative space, but not without its own autonomy.

OPPOSITE
Lyric Theatre
Belfast, 2011,
O'Donnell + Tuomey.

LEFT
Berlin Philharmonie,
1963, Hans Scharoun.

RIGHT
Irish Film Institute
Dublin, 1992.

Public Space

The foyer of the Irish Film Institute is a route as well as a place. Its spatial configuration comes from a string of spaces that lead like stepping stones from the street through to the heart of the building, to end in an outdoor room at the other side of the block. The high central space, with its railway-station glass roof, is intended to feel external, like a campo at the convergence of routes, overlooked by the balcony cafe and blind windows in the old brick walls. A lot of energy comes from the pull of the new against the old, repurposed rooms imposing their geometry on a general purpose space.

We can call it a campo because this kind of plan-making, between side-stepping places and shifting routes, is very Venetian in character, practical lessons learned from walking through that city, applied not only from analysis of maps and plans but from personal experience of spatial conditions, observing how people occupy places and move through interlocking paths. It's the repetition of similar but never identical sequences that allows for their assimilation into our ways of working. Venice is the city of poignant absences, empty spaces that seem to hold the ghost of a spectacle, one you've just managed to miss. How can that feeling of presence be captured in a static structure? Is it to do with surprising shifts in direction, entering the campo in one corner and finding the exit is rarely opposite, reinforcing the sense of enclosure in its intimate interior before moving on? Or is it because these traffic-free spaces have dimensions normally found inside buildings? The ten-minute walk from the Accademia to the Frari is a sequence of narrow compression and angled release, culminating in the Calle Stretta Lipoli, apparently a dead-end, but then a crack opens—through which looms the brick bulk of the church—and another series of spaces begins to open up. That tiny gap measures less than one metre wide. On a drawing it would look wrong, yet the whole throng of Venice moves freely through it. If that urban shift had been designed with input from traffic-flow analysts or desk-bound advisors, the gap would be four metres wide and all the drama would be lost.

The IFI, our first public building, was designed to weave a path through a tangle of historic urban fabric. It made a new place out of a semi-derelict city block. Our next project was for the fully derelict half of that same block, a cultural space for events and performance. While the IFI was still on site, the Group 91 collective won the competition for the Temple Bar Framework Plan and, eventually, poachers-turned-gamekeepers, working with like-minded friends and colleagues on Dublin's cultural quarter, we designed two buildings across from each other on Meeting House Square, two buildings connected by an immaterial idea. Cinema can be projected from a box built into the National Photography Archive onto a screen housed in the window of the Gallery of Photography. On the other axis, theatre can be performed on a stage opened from inside to outside. The square has the characteristics of an internal space. It is a gathering space for the four institutions which surround it, a weekend food market and a quiet pocket space away from the hustle of the city.

In these early works we developed a lasting aspiration that public buildings, with loose-fit permeable plans, with suites of in-between spaces, should feel like natural extensions of the space of the city, indoor-outdoor places open to the civic realm,

OPPOSITE LEFT
Calle Stretta Lipoli, Venice.

OPPOSITE RIGHT
Three projects in Temple Bar superimposed on 1847 Ordnance Survey map of Dublin.

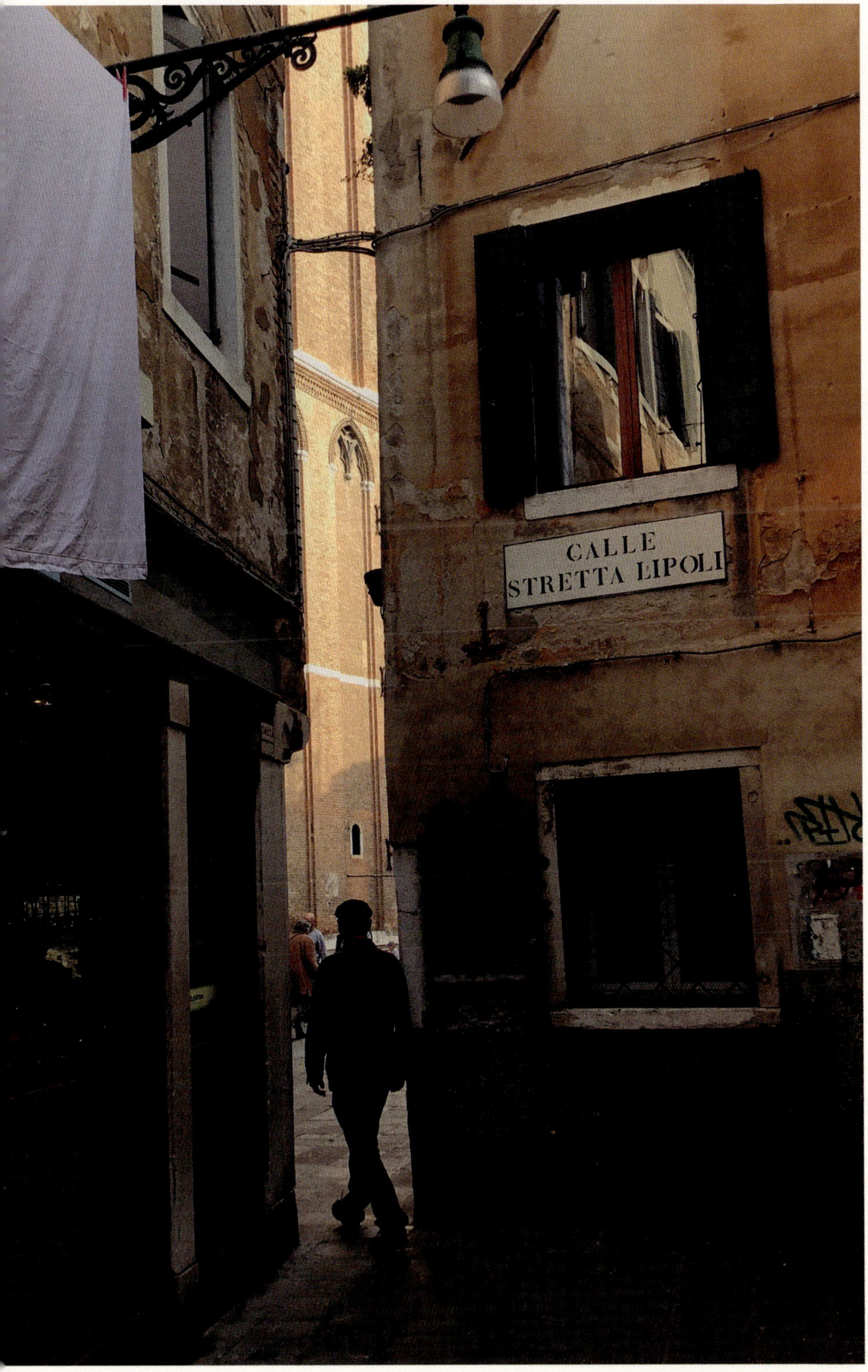

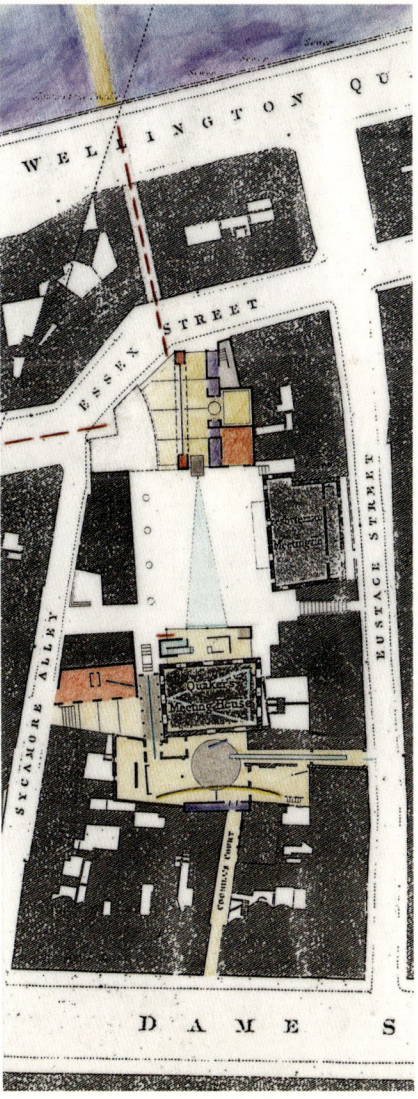

Public Space 203

like the old railway-station halls. This thinking runs through all our cultural-cluster buildings: the Lyric Theatre in Belfast, the Irish Language Centre in Derry, the Sean O'Casey Centre, the Central European University in Budapest. In the eight-storey student centre at the London School of Economics, the staircase itself, with its landings and hallways, becomes the public space. The site is small; the uses are many and public in nature. The stair varies in width and pace as it twists up through the building, sometimes opening to adjacent spaces, sometimes enclosed, always landing back at the fixed point of the lift shaft—as if one of the narrow medieval lanes that run through the open street campus had wound itself around a multicoloured totem pole.

All these projects prepared us to move up a scale. We had learned to act strategically and think experientially at the same time. We realised that every house needs an urban strategy and every city block needs intimate space. When the chance came

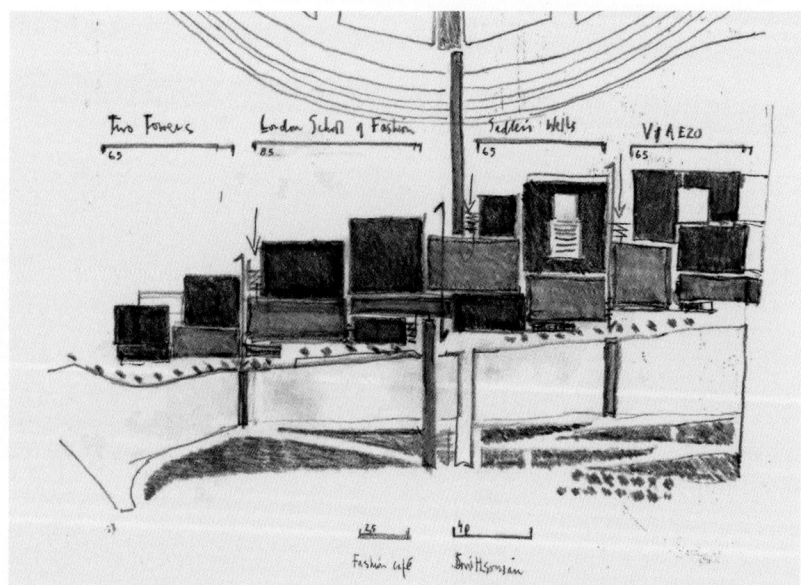
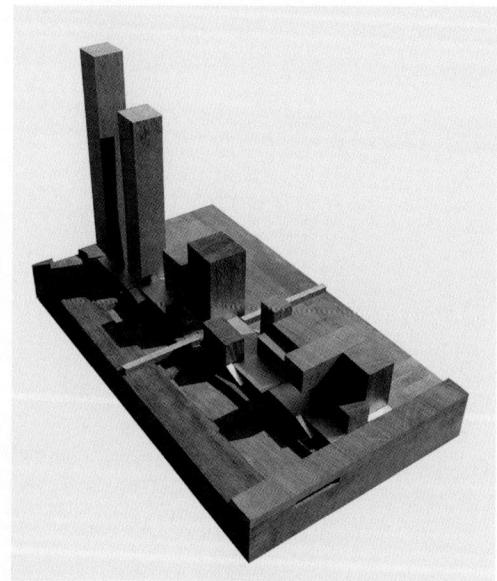

LEFT
Olympicopolis masterplan study sketch.

RIGHT
Woodblock and gold-leaf model, Olympicopolis design stage, O'Donnell+Tuomey.

to design a new cultural, educational and residential quarter in East London, we were ready.

Towards the end stages of construction at the LSE, I was on the Tube to Heathrow, as usual, at the end of a long working day, wondering where our next job would come from. I happened on an article in the *Evening Standard*, the announcement of an international competition on the site of the London Olympics. The so-called *Olympicopolis*, a civic-minded project inspired by London's West End museum district known as *Albertopolis*, would include a new museum for the V&A, a design school for UCL, a theatre, and residential and other cultural buildings. I was stopped in my tracks, though the train kept going. This was it. The dream job, just right for us, the next step exactly. I tore the page out of the newspaper and, on the plane, showed it to John. He thought I was crazy—surely everyone would be after

More Space for Architecture

that job. But, somehow, I knew it was for us. I brought the torn-out page back to the office and kept an eye out for further information.

The competition sought teams of architects, with different strengths and experience. We proposed a collaborative team, combining together with Allies and Morrison from London and Arquitecturia from Girona. A+M with its extensive experience in urban master planning, Arquitecturia an emerging practice, together with our experience in cultural and educational buildings, and all of us familiar with complex urban settings. It worked as a team, with values held in common, and with each practice bringing its own culture and individual outlook. What was similar was the shared aspiration for connections between public institutions, an inclination to involve both internal and external spaces in the architectural concept. When we first contacted them, we had forgotten that Allies and Morrison had been quite so closely involved with the Olympics. The *Olympicopolis* suggested a different approach, a different urban density. Bob Allies suggested that we should lead on the early stages of the masterplan.

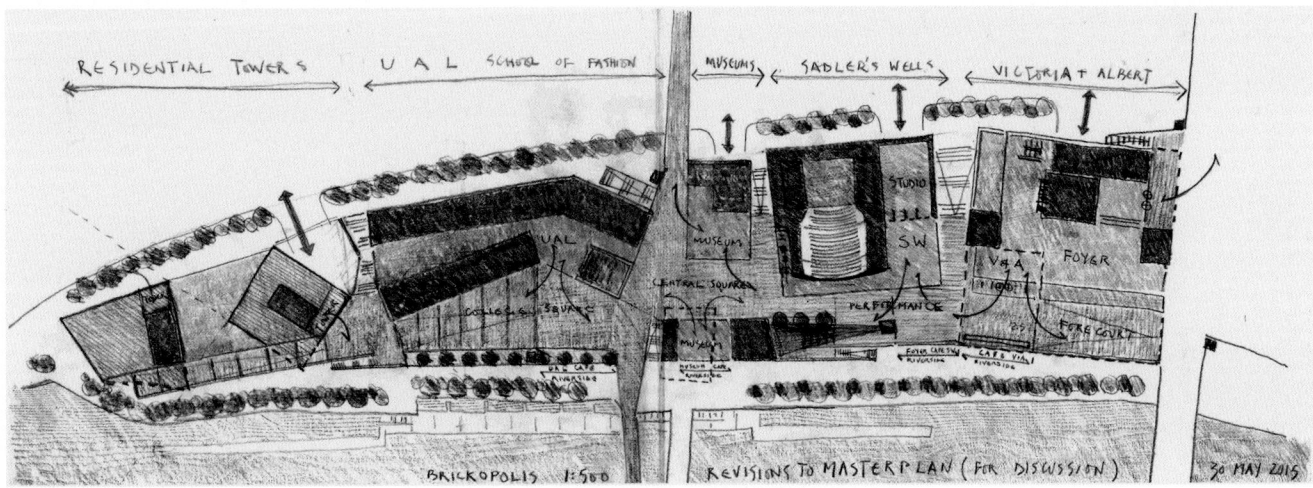

The site is a narrow strip of land bordered on the south by the River Lea and the Olympic Park and on the north by a busy road and multiple railway tracks. Beyond the railway the new International Quarter adjoins Westfield shopping centre, separating the competition site from the old neighbourhoods of Stratford, from ordinary urban city fabric. The brief included the V&A, Sadler's Wells Dance Theatre, the London College of Fashion, the BBC studios, 600 apartments and an emphasis on open civic space to encourage social engagement. The residential density made it clear it would be necessary to build high. The variety of independent institutions meant there could not be a singular or homogenous urban form.

The site was disconnected, not only in plan but also in section, from its neighbourhood surroundings. A legacy of the Olympics was that elevated parcels of land, connected by bridges and overpasses, allowed for easy pedestrian movement during the games, while vital transport connections continued to operate on the network

ABOVE
Olympicopolis masterplan study sketch.

of rail and roads below. Stratford enjoys excellent public transport to central London and the world beyond, but those very corridors cut it off from easy local connections. The masterplan had to facilitate pedestrian movement from west to east across an eight-metre level change, while providing universal access to all the new buildings.

The competition called for a masterplan, but in reality it's more like an urban design, with not much generic about the final scheme. It's not a loose-fit strategy of adaptable streets and blocks. It's a three-dimensional puzzle that connects an isolated piece of ground, the size and shape of an aircraft carrier, to its hinterland, that connects the constituent parts to each other. This is done through the placement of purpose-designed buildings which, inside and out, help to navigate complex level changes in the public realm. The whole site is a stretched-out triangle, high above ground at its wider west end, where it connects to the broad pedestrian route from Westfield to the Stadium, narrowing down to street level at the east end, leading to Hackney Wick and Fish Island.

Having won the competition, we faced the immediate challenge of having to move everything around. For phasing and for commercial reasons, our proposed location of residential structures at the middle of the site was not viable. However, the overall design proposal survived various rounds of change and strategic review. The basic principle, of buildings and spaces shifting to form connections, proved itself capable of adaptation to a multitude of client and user demands.

We started, as we always do, by immersing ourselves in the context. We took windswept walks where we always seemed to be looking down from high-level bridges at fenced-in parcels of land, at rail tracks, roads and cut-off waste ground. In the background were the construction sites of the new International Quarter, the huge shopping centre, several monumental buildings from the Olympics, none of these yet settled into the foreground. And the great relief of the Queen Elizabeth Olympic Park, which was quietly maturing and becoming more beautiful, one piece of legacy instantly integrated. We turned to historic maps to trace the memory of previous industrial structures on this transitional site. The cross-grain of the site, running from railway to river, had been erased in the construction of a temporary water polo arena. It really was a *tabula rasa*.

The cultural institutions are themselves deeply connected, woven into the creative fabric of London, national institutions with international reputations. Their new buildings will offer exciting opportunities for novel experimental work, specific to their setting in London's East End. And working together, they can make new multi-disciplinary projects that respond positively to their co-location. Cultural continuity and transport connections are assured, allowing everyone to get on with their work in conditions closely designed to their requirements. Time will be the judge of whether the combination of uses, together with the character of the place itself, can generate the wished-for public engagement and social interaction. For us, as architects, this seven-year project has been a rare challenge and well worth the effort. You have to make the work you believe in, and you have to stick with it.

OPPOSITE
Stratford Waterfront, elevation to the park, with O'Donnell + Tuomey projects in red.

+ The Prow

SHADOWS AND LIGHT

This tower of apartments sits in a prominent position in the East Bank residential masterplan, on its narrow tapered prow, at the northern tip of the new education and cultural district. It has a monolithic presence, marking a point of arrival from Hackney Wick, transitional between the new urban density and the more open landscape of parkland and train tracks. The symmetrical form fills the shape of its site, setting back in six-storey shifts to become more slender as it rises. Its pencil-like shape is designed to be seen in the round, standing in space, taking advantage of 360-degree views across the Queen Elizabeth Olympic Park.

A hexagonal plan allows all 130 apartments to enjoy dual aspect views, a mixture of one-, two- and three-bedroom flats, each with a sheltered balcony and floor-to-ceiling bay windows. Angled walls allow daylight deep into the building. The apartment plans share a common list of ingredients, with bathrooms and services rationally arranged around a hexagonal core, but each with a different outlook.

The 24-storey facade is constructed from precast concrete, rough textured and pigmented sandstone-red. This triple-storey order brings measure and scale. The solid skin is manipulated to enhance plasticity, inspired by the terracotta treatment of typical East London mansion blocks. Faceted wall panels provide depth in the wall, creating lively conditions of shadow and light across the undulating surface of the elevation. Recessed balconies rotate around the building in active response to orientation and urban outlook. The loggia-type balconies and open terraces enjoy long-range views in all directions across the wider landscape. The scale of the building changes as it hits the ground, with civic functions facing the pedestrian path along the River Lea.

FRONTISPIECE
Entrance from waterfront.

TOP
River Lea Walk.

BOTTOM
Massing studies with Allies and Morrison.

OPPOSITE TOP
East Bank elevation to the park.

OPPOSITE BOTTOM
Carpenters Road, River Lea.

OVERLEAF
East Bank viewed from the park.

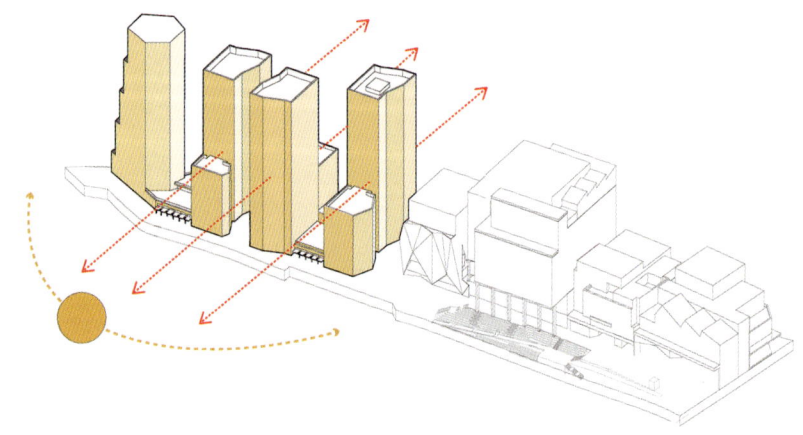

210   More Space for Architecture

Public Space

211

Public Space

+ Sadler's Wells Dance Theatre and Studios
READY FOR WORK

This building is for dance in all its forms: performance, composing and experimenting. It houses a flexible dance theatre, a centre for choreography and a hip-hop academy. Sited at the entrance to Eastbank, it makes a bookend to the park-facing terrace of cultural buildings, where all are welcome. Public entry is from two sides on the pedestrian podium. Eight metres below podium, the stage door and get-in are at street level on Carpenters Road.

It's a square building with an orderly plan. The auditorium holds the street corner and its flytower rises the full height. Six studios wrap around the flytower in two ranges at upper levels. Below the studios, the free-flowing L-shaped foyer is a public living room with cafe, bars and a community dance platform. These activities extend outside under a deep portico which gives shade and shelter, an eyebrow over the entrance.

The form is influenced by dance notation, where alternating black and white feet are arranged in a static diagram of movement. The individual parts, derived from the fixed dimensions and rectangular requirements of the brief, are expressed in a rhythmic composition around the square block of the flytower. The Aurelian walls of ancient Rome, with their rows of projecting towers, helped us to find a language for the massing of the unfenestrated flytower.

The character of the building is in keeping with the industrial past of the site. Walls and roofs are clad in brick and big tiles made of the same purple-ish clay. On one side it is a brick monolith: a solid sculpted mass with corbelled chimney and articulated staircase. Brickwork steps and chamfers to form entrances, articulate surfaces and turn corners. The sawtooth studios enliven the skyline.

It's a straightforward building, designed to be open, welcoming and ready for work.

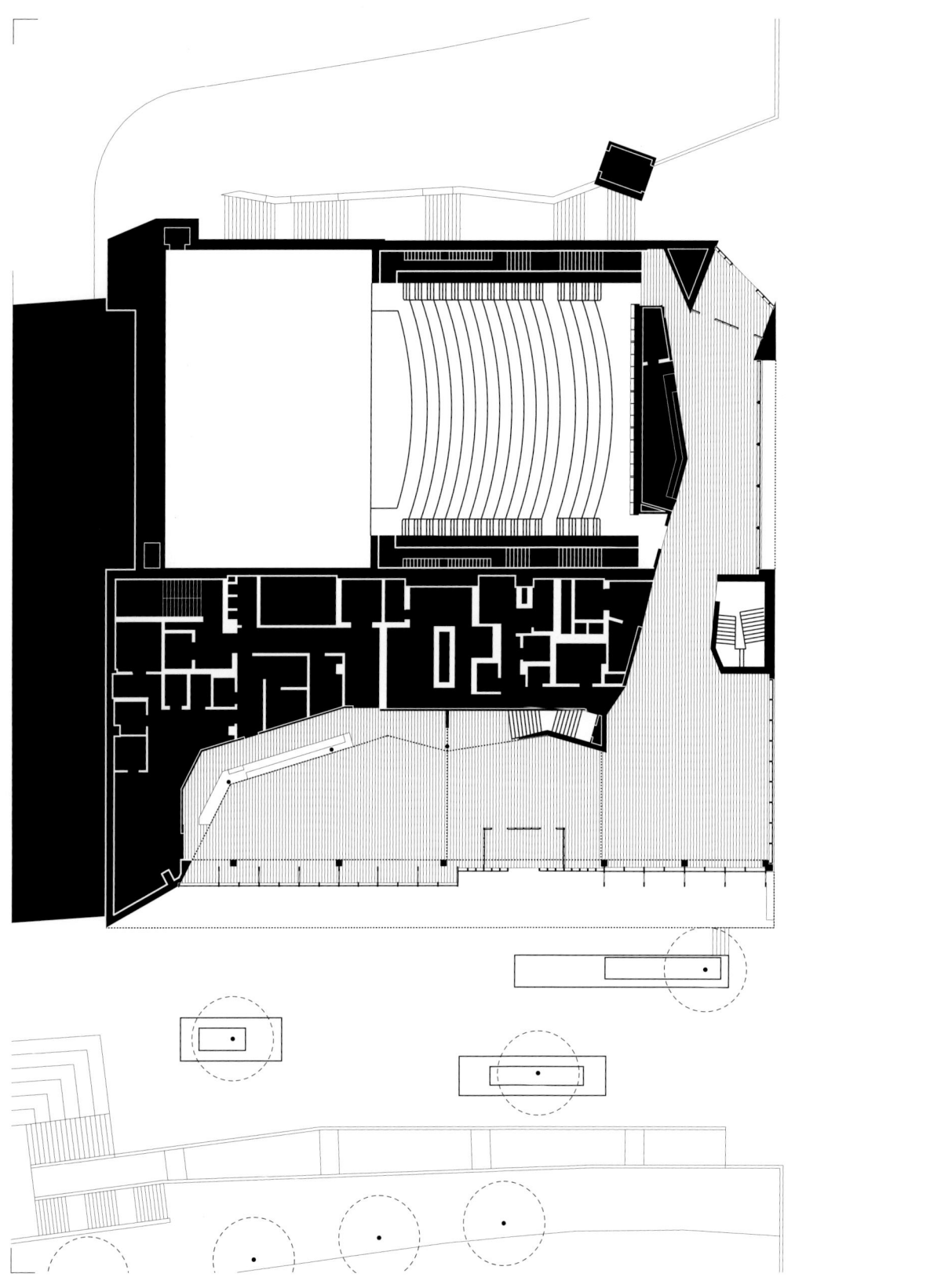

FRONTISPIECE
Theatre and large studio.

OPPOSITE
Plan, scale 1:450.

TOP
View from the bridge.

BOTTOM
Foyer sketch.

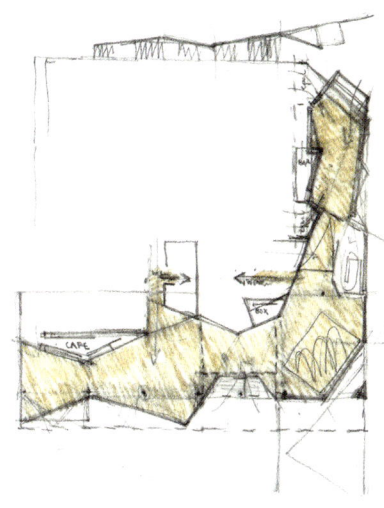

Public Space 217

illustrative concept sketch

10.8.17

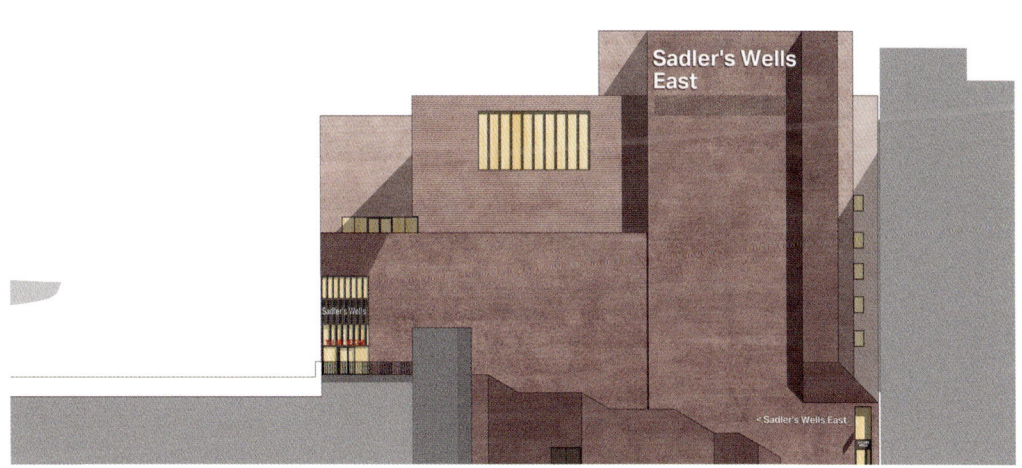

OPPOSITE
Watercolour study.

TOP
Elevation to the park.

MIDDLE
Street elevation.

BOTTOM
Concrete model/
pencil holder.

OVERLEAF
Approach from
Stratford Walk.

Public Space

Sited at the entrance to Eastbank, it makes a bookend to the park-facing terrace of cultural buildings, where all are welcome. Public entry is from two sides on the pedestrian podium. Eight metres below podium, the stage door and get-in are at street level on Carpenters Road.

Public Space

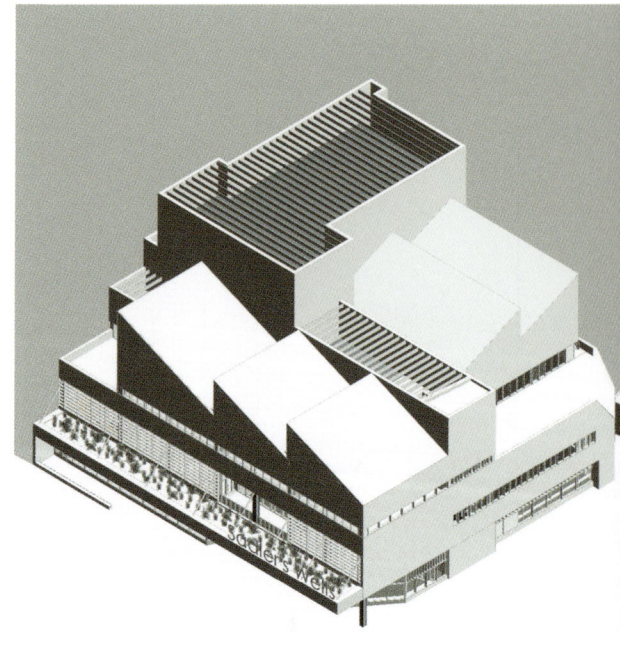

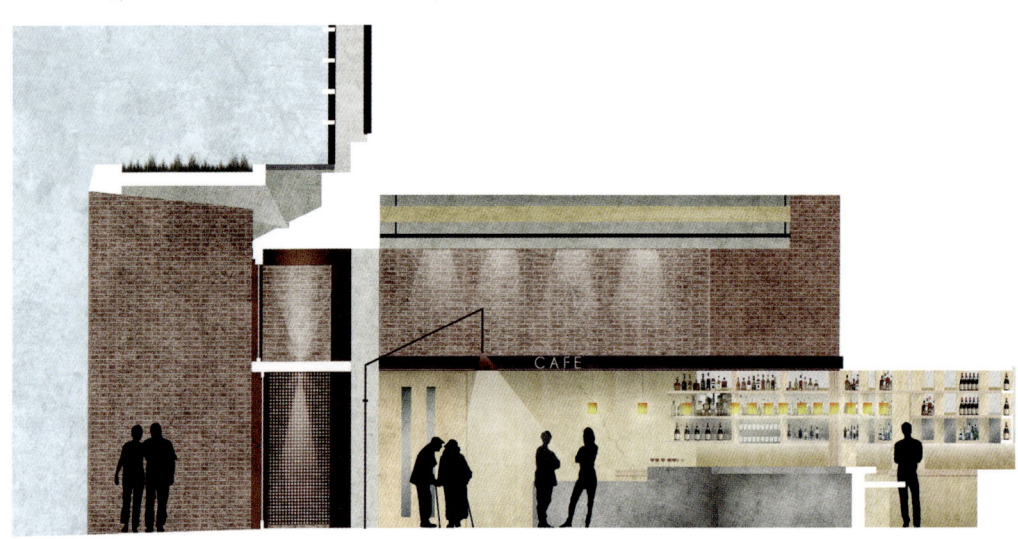

TOP LEFT
Foyer section perspective.

TOP RIGHT
Dance studios, sawtooth roofscape.

BOTTOM RIGHT
Foyer section, canopy study.

OPPOSITE
Upper floor plan, scale 1:450. Dance studios and flytower void.

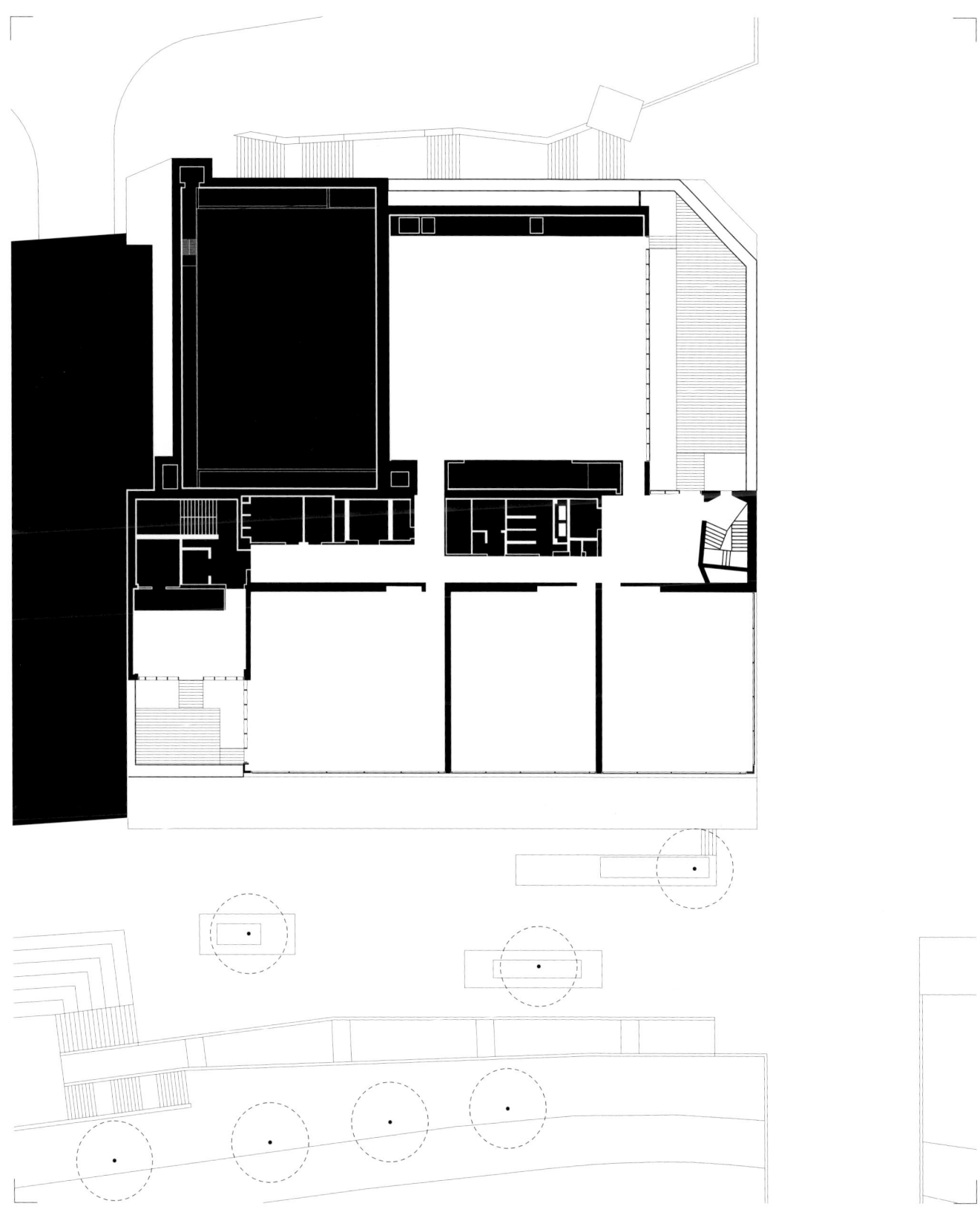

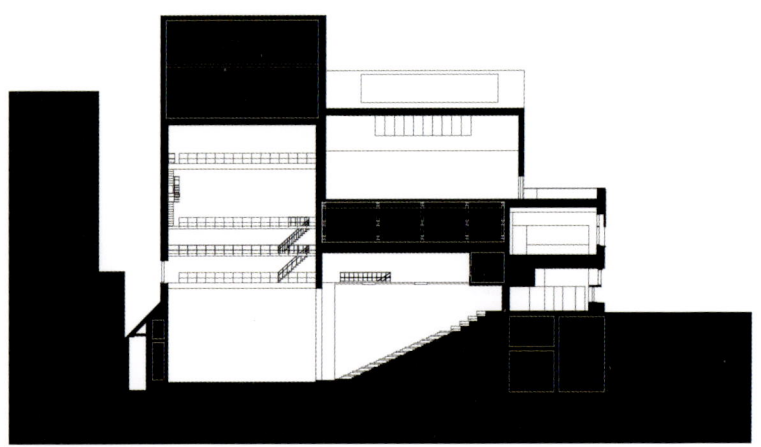

FROM TOP
Cross-section, theatre and large studio; Cross-section, foyer and studios; Section study, theatre and large studio.

OPPOSITE TOP
View from the south.

OPPOSITE BOTTOM
Foyer study, section perspective.

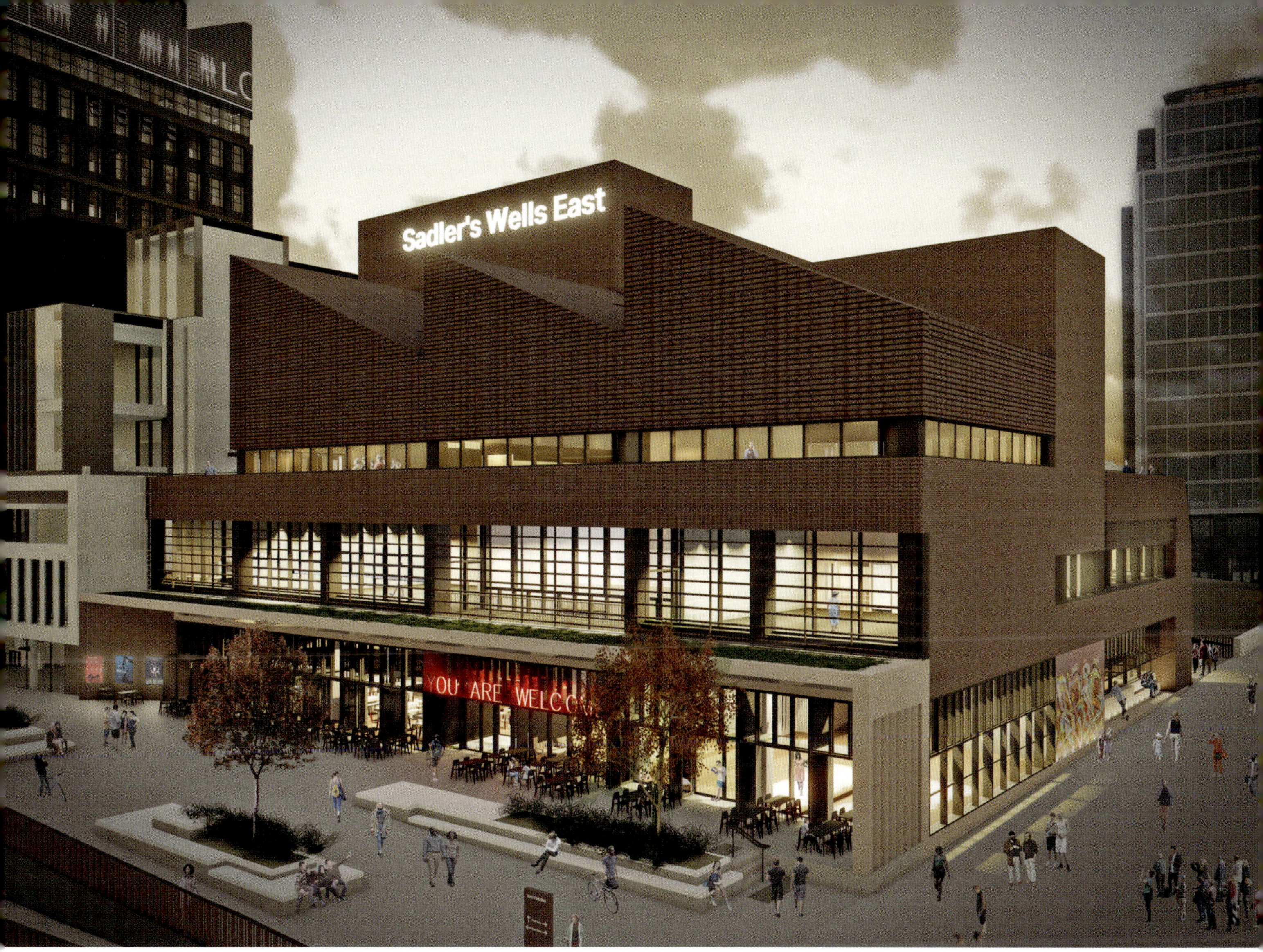

Public Space

225

+ V&A East

A NEW MUSEUM

A new museum in East London where visitors can explore different aspects of the V&A's collection and experience contemporary art, design and performance. The programme will be co-curated with the Smithsonian Institution, bringing these two museums together for the first time.

The building will house exhibitions, gallery displays, events and activities, spaces for community-led projects, installations and collaborations—with a cafe, shop, outdoor public spaces and views over the Queen Elizabeth Olympic Park from a public roof terrace. The five-storey museum has two public entrances: from podium level and from the waterfront square. Designed around a central core, the galleries lead one to another in sequence, inviting visitors to explore the entire building, with a large space on the third floor for temporary exhibitions.

The V&A 2017 Balenciaga exhibition had a memorable display that drew attention to the Spanish couturier's use of the Japanese concept of 'Ma' or the space in between. His sculptural garments provide a sense of space between the body and the enclosing fabric—framing rather than restricting the figure. Study sketches of similar sleeve spaces in Vermeer's *Woman Writing a Letter* were another useful reference point in our discussions of the architectural idea for the V&A East.

The skin of the building acts as a three-dimensional folded form, 'the jacket itself', giving identity to the museum and a protective coat for the environmentally controlled conditions within. The faceted facade is built in crafted concrete, prefabricated in 464 individually tailored and interlocking pieces, stacked in two-metre bandwidths, each panel different, drawn all over with overlapping lines of low relief. Mural stairs and viewing windows occupy the thickness of the outer crust.

228 More Space for Architecture

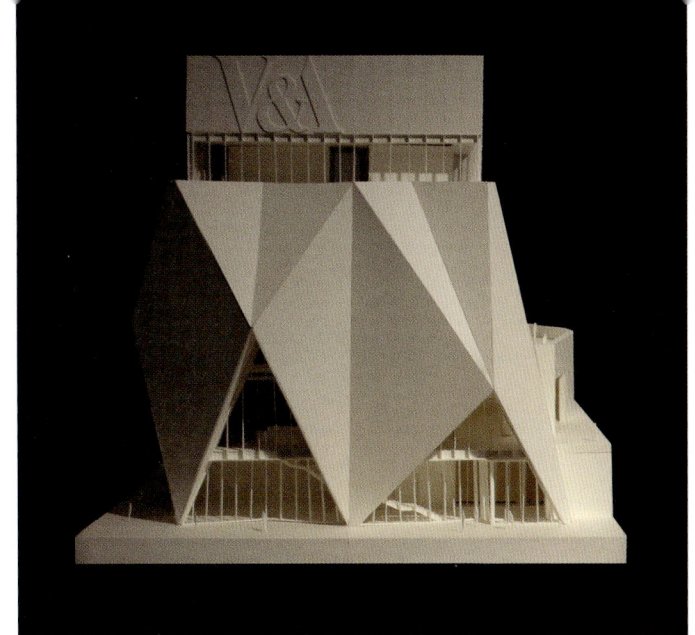

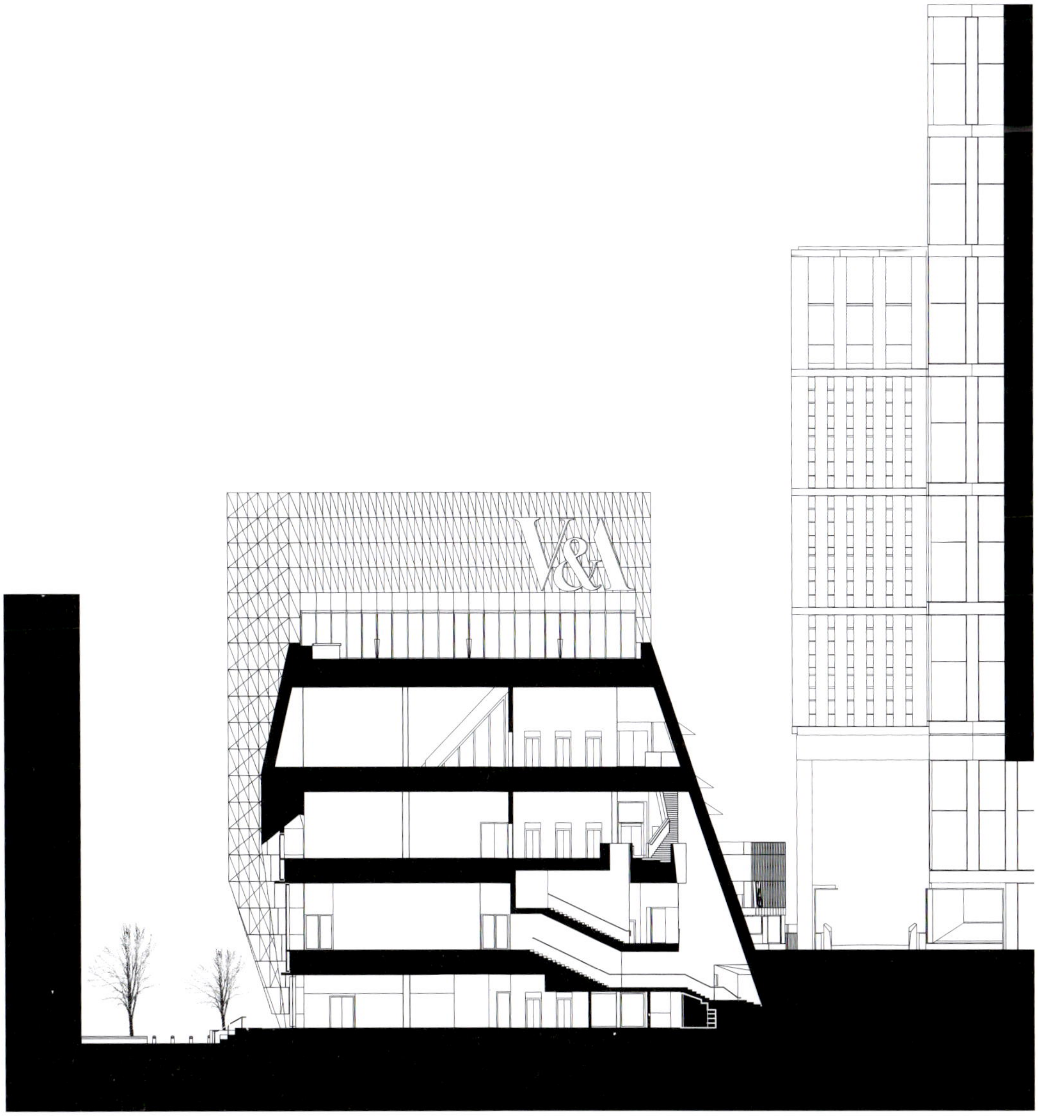

FRONTISPIECE
View from the park.

OPPOSITE
Wall thickness study, section model.

TOP
Card study model.

BOTTOM
Cross-section.

Public Space

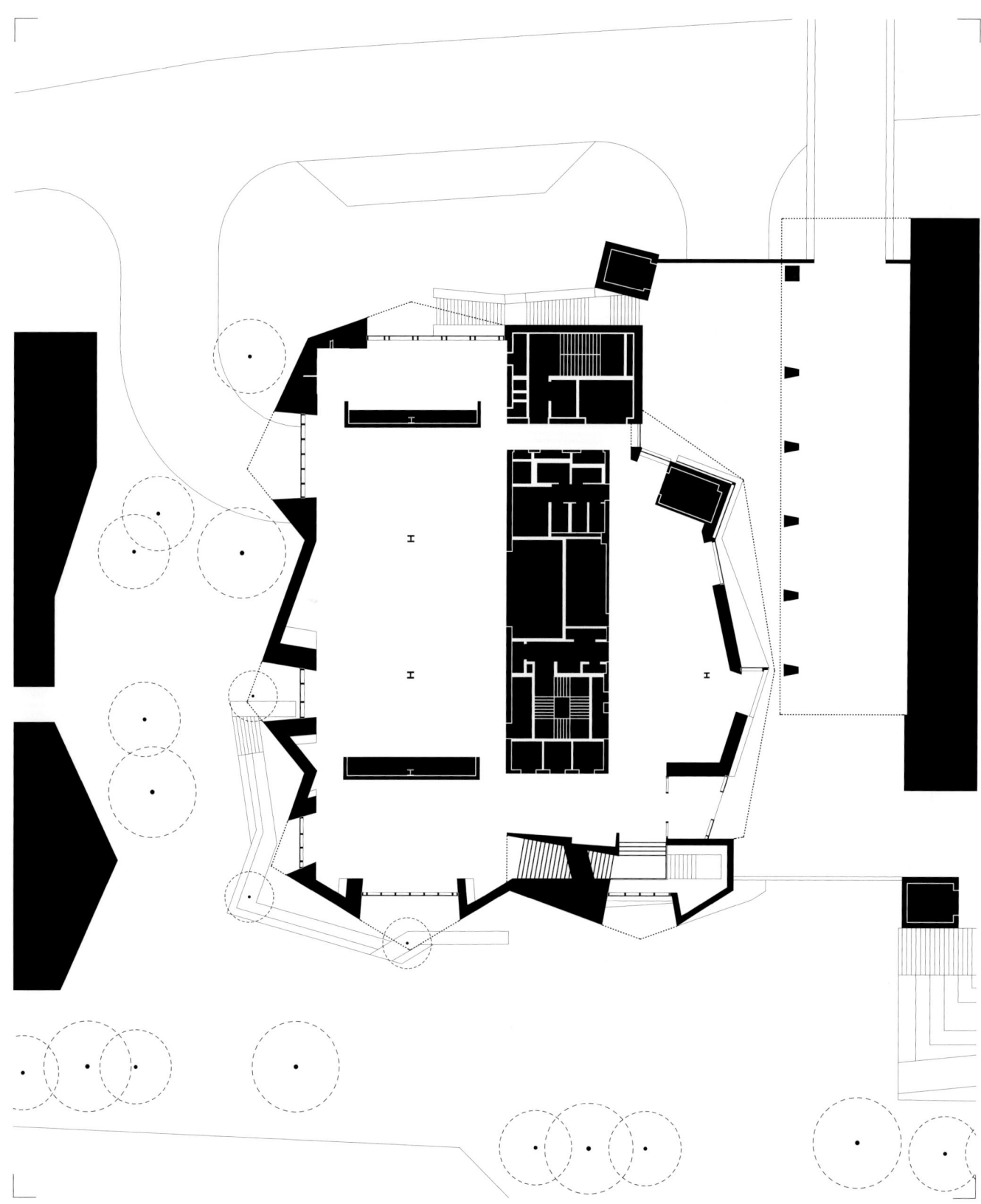

OPPOSITE
Plan, scale 1:450.

TOP
View to the park.

BOTTOM
Site section.

OVERLEAF
Waterfront Square, entrance and cafe.

Public Space

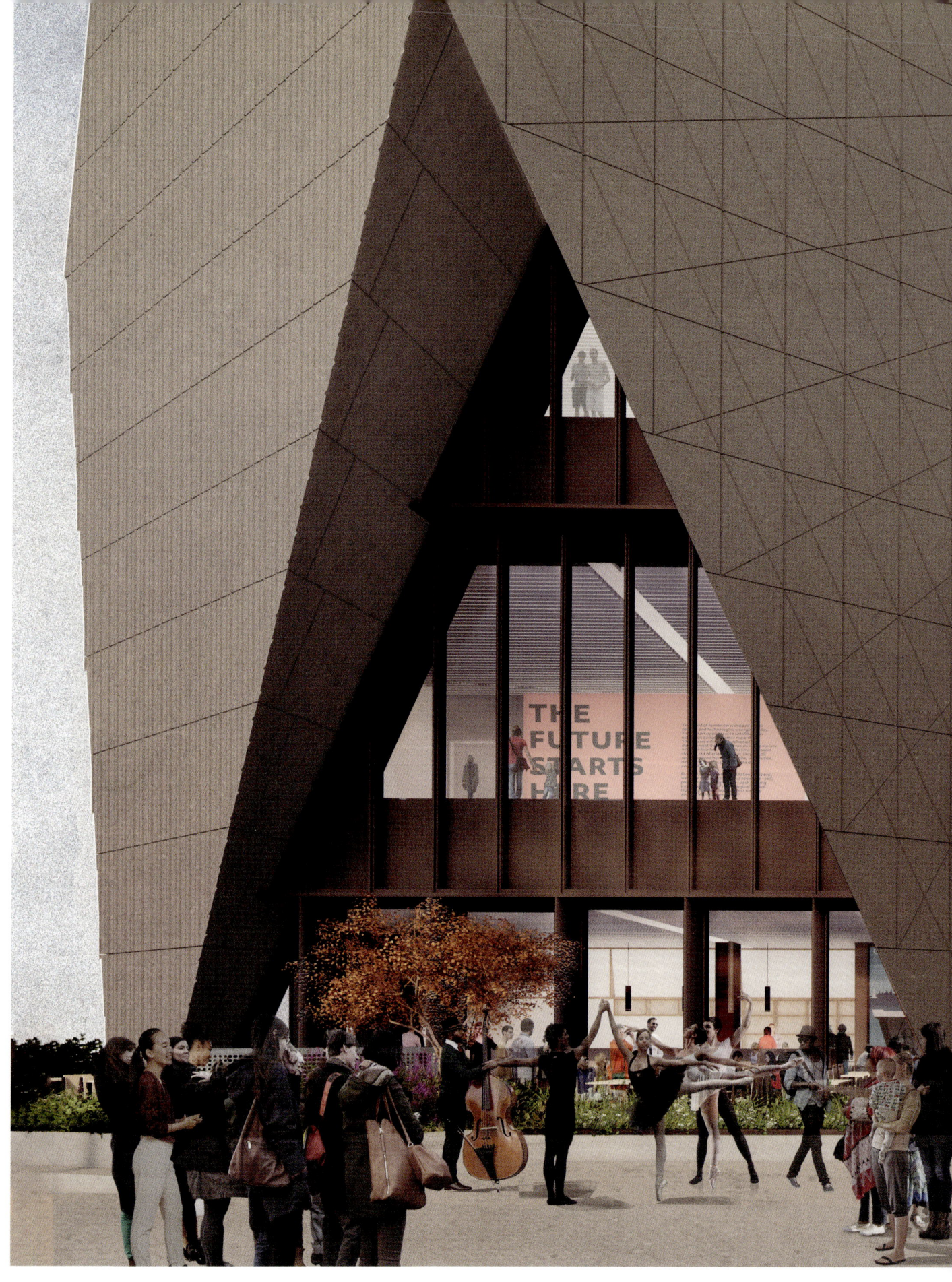

Public Space

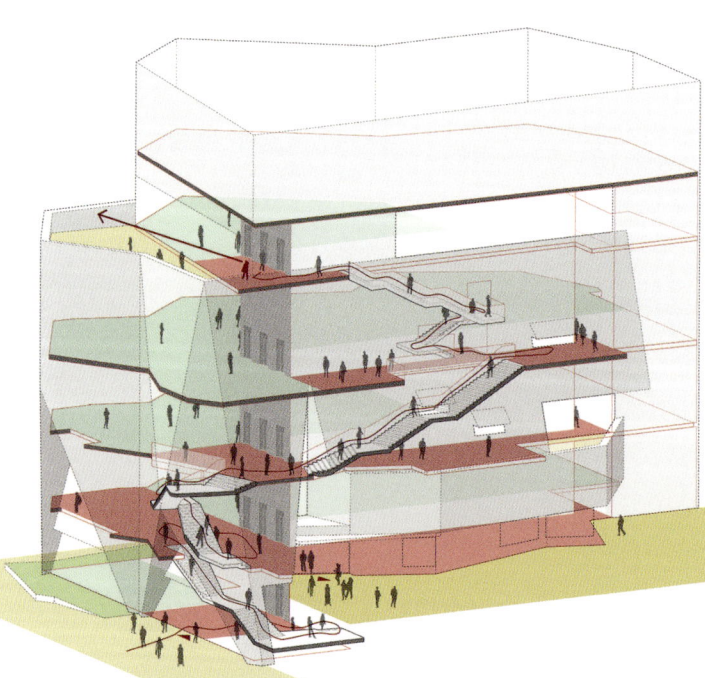

TOP
Precast concrete profile, test sample.

BOTTOM
Visitor journey diagram.

OPPOSITE
Upper floor plan, scale 1:450. Exhibition galleries and office areas.

234 More Space for Architecture

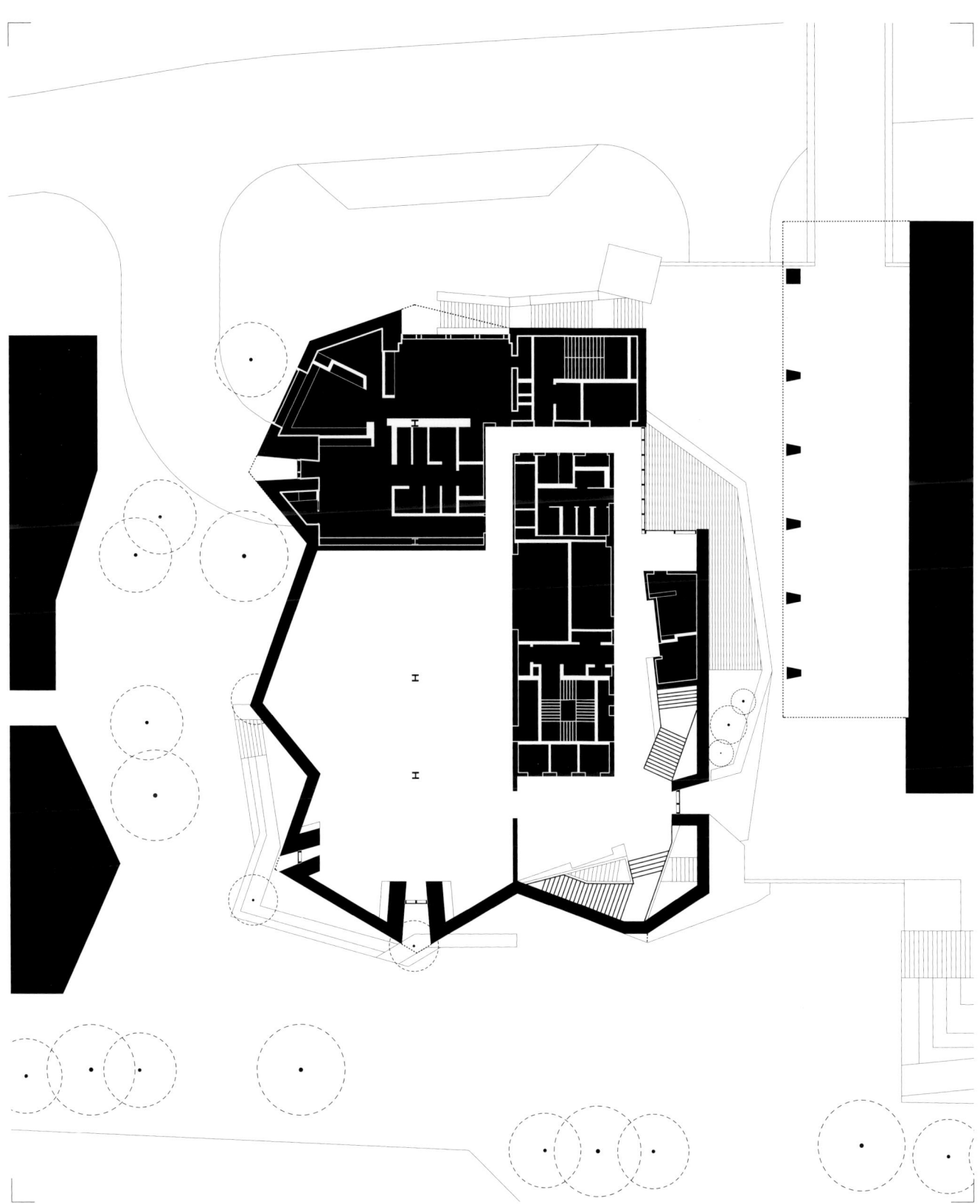

Public Space

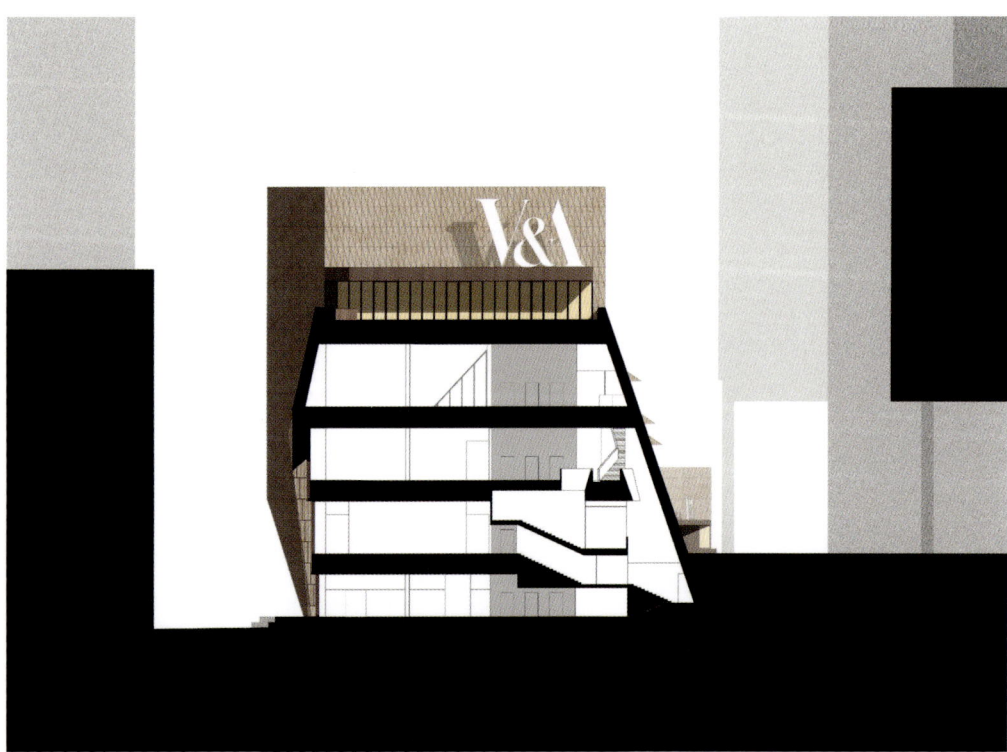

TOP
Waterfront Square elevation.

BOTTOM
Cross-section.

OPPOSITE TOP
Triptych: Balenciaga Black Silk Evening Gown, 1967, photographed by Cecil Beaton; Balenciaga Dress X-ray print by Nick Veasey, V&A Archives; V&A East Museum elevation X-ray, O'Donnell + Tuomey.

OPPOSITE BOTTOM
Podium level gallery, isometric study.

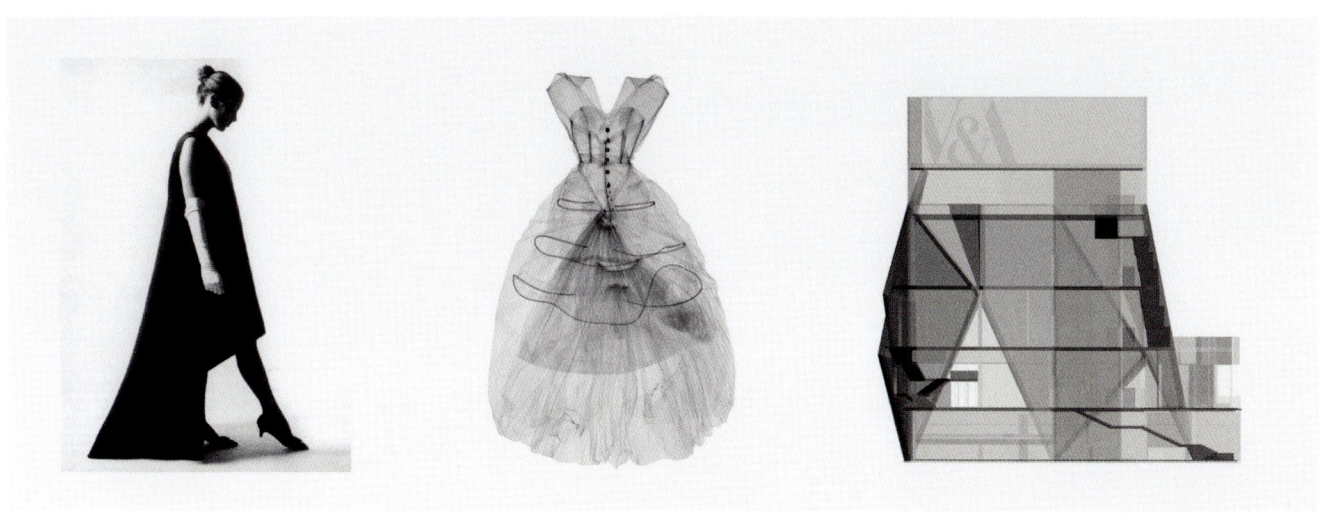

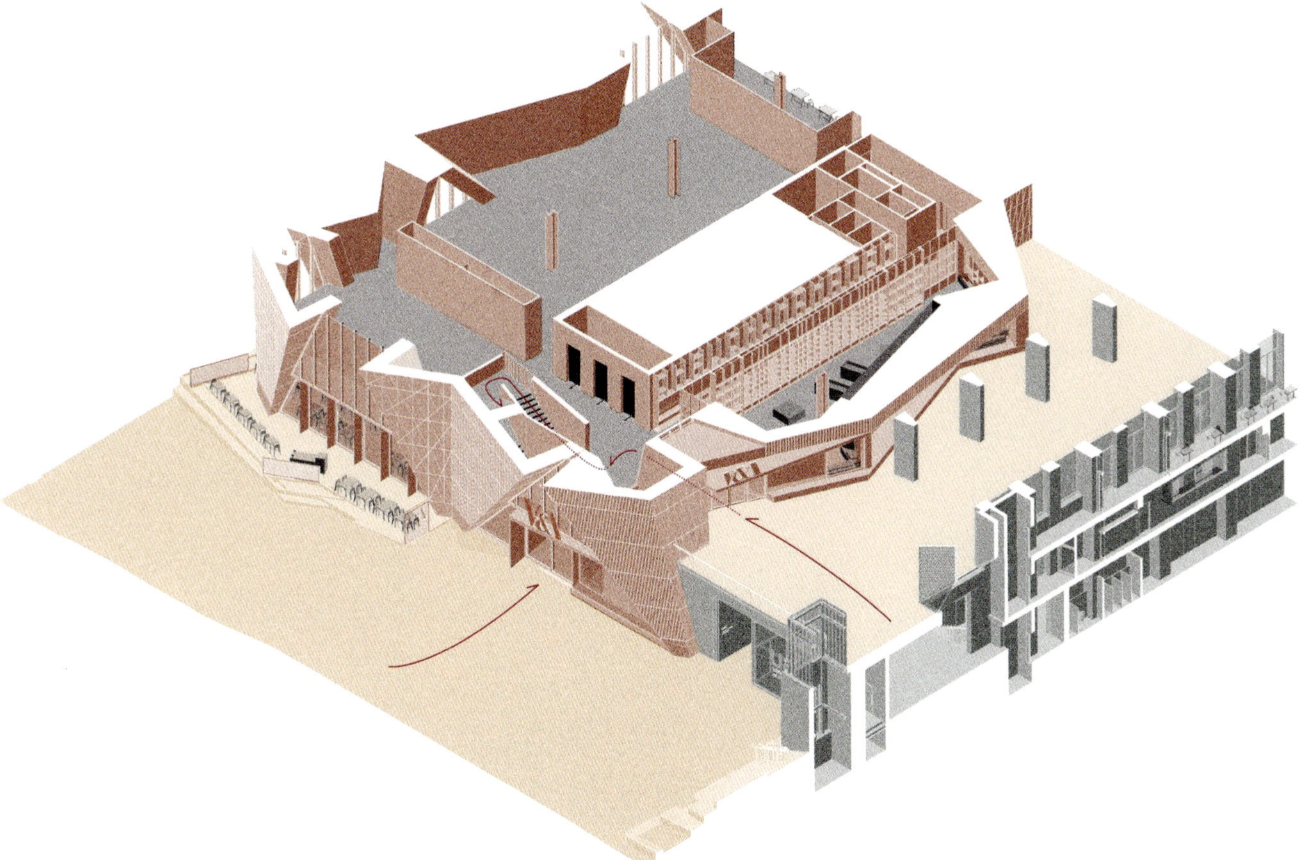

Public Space

Space, Volume, Structure

Whhen we look for the origins of the Greek temple we find that the setting comes first, long before the building. A promontory, a spring of water, a cave, a grove of trees—any unusual or life-giving phenomenon could seem to possess an unseen power.

BLUE GUIDE TO GREECE, THE ANCIENT GREEK TEMPLE

According to the *Blue Guide to Greece*, and we should remember that this is a guide for the general reader and not aimed only at architects, there are three primary elements needed to define most ancient places of cult: the table that marks the spot, the perimeter that defines its setting and the chamber that houses the goods. Greek architecture is all about the outside, the vital presence of the object. If we were reading from a yet-to-be-written *Blue Guide to the Byzantine* it would have been all about the interior luminous space. Combining these two tendencies, the search for external presence and the exploration of internal volume, to be found in the concrete clarity of the foundations at Delphi and the

brick-built mysteries of Hagia Sophia, perhaps we could be seen as much more Greco-Byzantine in our spiritual origins, and not be wrongly perceived as some species of roving Irish regionalists.

The Letterfrack furniture workshops were an experiment in consequential stages of construction, starting with site preparation, then structural concrete, followed by timber-frame assembly. Only then, with the raw skeleton in place, could works be coordinated with different trades together. On such a remote site, it made sense to revert to traditional strategies, masonry structures built months ahead of carpentry completions. In Letterfrack, the concrete subcontractors were long gone before the next gang arrived to set out their trusses on the empty slabs. The building bears witness to this layered process, concrete clear of the ground, timber bolted to concrete haunches, green oak cladding clamped to the gables. The logic stays legible in the experience of space, volume, structure. Twenty years later, that strategy is being tested again at the new school of architecture in Liverpool.

OPPOSITE
Furniture College
Letterfrack, 2001,
O'Donnell+Tuomey.

LEFT
Hagia Sofia, Istanbul,
interior volume.

RIGHT
Altar of Aphrodite,
Athens.

Space, Volume, Structure

In the Glucksman Gallery, with the River Lee cutting through a limestone escarpment, we worked our way upwards and out of the ground of the site. The project began in plan and developed in section as a consequence of the first move. Then the form developed in a non-linear way, or in a series of jumps, as it were, from the first line drawn in the sand, in this case helped by leaning on Seamus Heaney's poem "Lightenings viii. The annals say". For this secluded riverside site, our first thoughts were to keep all the existing trees, to lift the gallery up in the air, up above the limestone escarpment, to turn the plan to look out from the gallery, to focus on selected views of the college in one direction and back to the city along and not across the river. The Glucksman has a void at its centre, an inverted courtyard that has been pushed up from below. The inner section is made visible in the external form.

At the Irish Language Centre in Derry, we worked our way outwards from within a landlocked infill site. The courtyard is treated like a residual volume remaining after the extraction of some imagined medieval tower house, a solid spatial volume rather than a negative void. The plan opens up a three-dimensional civic processional journey, with the visitor moving up through the building section like the ball in a pinball machine, propelled along their journey by incidents encountered in their path. Overlapping spaces overlook the route through the various levels of this very public building.

The external expression of the Lyric Theatre was developed from the tradition of Belfast brick buildings. But at the centre of the internal public streetscape is another project entirely, the tiered timber auditorium, an acoustic vessel, embodying the

RIGHT
Furniture College Letterfrack, timber-frame structure.

active interdependence between actor and audience. Between the auditorium and the street, the building form opens up to extend its interior volumes out towards the river landscape.

Aalto, Borromini, Kahn and the Question of Form

> In making a poem you have no right to think of anything but the subject matter; after making it no right to boast of anything but the form.
> ELIZABETH SHEPLEY SERGEANT, ROBERT FROST: THE TRIAL BY EXISTENCE

At the beginning of our studies at UCD, we have to admit to having taken little interest in Aalto, most probably put off by the unfinished imperfection of his buildings as objects. We spent a lot of our student days hiding out from unsympathetic tutors in the architecture library, following our noses through the bookstacks, through phases of immersion in English Brutalism, Russian Constructivism, learning about the mainstream masters Corb, Aalto and Kahn. To our inexperienced eyes, Aalto's buildings looked like lop-sided, gawky assemblages, their form weakened by not being honed to prismatic perfection. As a young architect, this struck me as a flaw, compared with the taut elegance of Le Corbusier's early white purism. I went on from UCD to the London office of James Stirling, whose own early works, the three red buildings, although undoubtedly gawky, and admittedly Aalto-influenced, tend to be whittled down in outline to a profiled three-dimensional clarity. Much later, on the occasion of an RIAI conference in Finland, we visited many of Aalto's masterworks and the scales fell from our previously prejudiced eyes. Like Saul, we could see again. I remember coming out from a bus opposite the House of Culture in Helsinki and being amazed by the fleshy, meaty redness of its material presence, with a profoundly physical free form and intensely active on the city street.

> What remains constant in Aalto's work is its drawing on the forms of the natural world to express growth and movement as a metaphor for human life.
> ALAN COLQUHOUN, MODERN ARCHITECTURE

Metaphor, the Greek word *meta* meaning the same as the Latin *trans*, means taking something from one place to another. In metaphor, as in translation, the meaning is carried across from one language to another, for instance, from everyday life into the art of architecture. An interesting aspect of Aalto's practice, and one that makes it particularly accessible to us now, is that the finished building form is rarely fully closed or completely sealed at the edges. Patrolling the ragged boundaries of an Aalto building in the round, some signs of the real and given world seem to intervene from beyond to prevent the work cohering into perfect self-containment, and so closing itself off from discourse with its necessary context. In Aalto's vision of order, something remains open and incomplete, like a frayed edge that allows us to see how the fabric is woven.

> ...and perhaps the greatest lyric poetry occurs where the naturalness of speech is only partly corseted by form, as in the best of Yeats.
> JOHN MONTAGUE, SHORT THOUGHTS ON THE LONG POEM

ABOVE
Glucksman Gallery, 2004, O'Donnell+Tuomey.

Space, Volume, Structure

Among his many natural gifts, Aalto had the happy gift of staying close to *the naturalness of speech,* drawing his inspiration from high and low culture, local barns as well as foreign temples. Based firmly in his home place, in the lakelands, islands and rocky terrain of Finland, he yearned all his life for the faraway, for the cities of Italy. He insisted that he needed to get to Italy regularly, to refresh his sense of life and his sources in architecture. In 1948, he somehow managed to convince the people of a small industrial island, centred around a plywood mill in the forest, that their new council chamber must rise higher than Siena town hall. Säynätsalo, *only partly corseted by form,* has no significant similarities with Siena, in style or culture, but its council chamber, at 17 metres, stands one metre higher than its counterpart in Siena, and that is a fact of which Säynätsalo remains proud. Not always such a showman, Aalto understood his work to make deep connections between the everyday and the exotic, to make a kind of elevated ordinary.

> Alvar Aalto began in Nordic classicism, which always had latent vernacular tendencies... even at his most severe, Aalto was softening the edges and disorganising the geometry.
>
> ROBERT HARBISON, TRAVELS IN THE HISTORY OF ARCHITECTURE

In the beautiful photograph of the free-form glass Savoy Vase 1936/7, beside its wooden mould, we witness the literal interdependence of the inner cast and the outer crust. Looking at the Vuoksenniska Church of the Three Crosses and at the section of the Maison Carrée, with this image of solid space in mind, we can see similar qualities, inner volumes strongly integrated with their external envelopes. Between both profiles, between the skin and the lining, lies a reserved space, an active thickness that can be light or dark, but never dormant. We can sense this same spatial tension, between within and without, along the line of the curved window wall that actively unites Aalto's Helsinki studio with its amphitheatrical garden, completed in 1956. This is sometimes referred to as a Baroque tendency, comparable to the lost space between the inner and outer domes of Borromini's churches, but it may be simpler to suggest that Aalto was building on something discovered through the method of his own design process, through continuous 6B pencil drawing, overlay sketches, painting composition, and many working models. The moulds that were used to press plywood into bent shapes produced positive results, but the resultant negative spaces themselves provided form-finding possibilities.

Aalto wrote about his approach to form in his influential essay "The Trout and the Stream". He provides access to his design process by way of analogy, restating a classical definition of the concept, something that is not *born fully grown,* but developed with difficulty, like a trout struggling upstream. Designs are gradually uncovered in the process of enquiry. Drawing, and long periods of parallel study, eventually lead through a process of conscious and unconscious crystallisation to

> ... an interweaving of the section and ground plan, and to a kind of unity of horizontal and vertical construction.
>
> ALVAR AALTO, THE TROUT AND THE STREAM

OPPOSITE
Lyric Theatre, watercolour competition sketch, 2003.

Space, Volume, Structure

In Aalto's best work the interior is nested loosely but inseparably inside its housing, like an animal inside its shell, or an instrument snugly fitting in its case. The notion of *unity* of form, to which Aalto aspires in *The Trout and the Stream,* is restated, in a more political context, in a later interview.

> Society is divided into factions, but I build for everybody. In other words, I must see society as a unity.

Having driven from Helsinki to Imatra, a long journey through the endless Finnish forest towards the Russian border, how strange on arrival at the Church of the Three Crosses to smell not incense or candles, but the scent of garage grease hanging in the air. The curved concrete doors, which slide away into the space between two skins, were designed to run on ball bearings in channels of oil. Aalto's published explanation would try to persuade us that for practical reasons the body of the church was divided into three parts. We are asked to believe that this was to allow for parish functions happening in parallel. We arrived just in time for a wedding, when the whole space was open as one. The wedding service seemed more civil than religious. We were witness to the light and acoustic scheme "working off each other", as Heaney might have us say. Aalto seems have been more interested in hollowing out the volume, moulding interior space to reflect light and sound, than in any specifically sacred atmosphere. He wanted the interior figure to develop its own form inside its exterior shell. Aalto seems to have designed in plan and section simultaneously. The sketches of Vuoksenniska and Maison Carré show this to be his habitual way of working. By this method, sketching out the ideas for his projects, he was scoping out, scooping out, the form. We can track this thinking back 20 years to the Savoy Vase, and ten years back from there, to his 1926 essay "From Doorstep to Living Room". Here he makes the case for an extended threshold between the exterior and interior experience of a building. Aalto uses Fra Angelico's fresco *The Annunciation* to illustrate the spirit of his argument, citing the reversed imagery of the angel in the garden and the virgin in the house. His interest lies in the ambiguous relationship between the spatial containment of the exterior and the sense of an interior instilled with the openness of the outside world.

> Turn your garden into an interior [...] make your hall into an "open air space"
> ALVAR AALTO, FROM DOORSTEP TO LIVING ROOM

In his later works, Aalto continued to explore the effects described by Soane as "lumière mystérieuse", the mystery of light finding its way through the reserved space held between layers, for instance in the marvellous rooflights of the Academic Bookshop. In the house of Louis Carré, art collector and patron to both Le Corbusier and Aalto, the central hall is treated like a public art gallery. The section steps gradually down with the hill. The roof slopes down in a single sweep with the lay of the land. But the spatial volume of the hall varies, rising and falling to allow daylight in from on high and glimpsed views out to the side.

Borromini's San Carlo alle Quattro Fontane was designed 300 years before the Savoy Vase, and then there was a 30-year gap between the interior construction

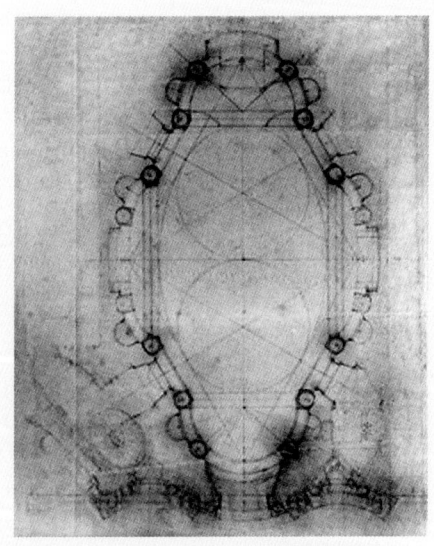

ABOVE
San Carlo alle Quattro Fontane, 1634, design drawing by Francesco Borromini.

and the completion of its street facade. We can imagine how Aalto must have loved this space; he might have thought its plan was made for him to play with. Let us approach one plan through another, to see the large scale connected to the small, to arrive at this tiny building like a clearing in the forest. The Nolli plan of Rome is much more than a map. It is a selective analysis of the vital organs of the city itself. It celebrates the interdependent relationship of urban volume to civic space. The continuous social space of Rome, with its churches, porticos and palazzo courtyards, reads as if it was carved out of the map's diagonally hatched background

density. As if all of the elements of the eternal city had emerged from a dark and solid mass, with each pocketed piazza and every cavernous passageway once having been scraped into existence out of the inky blackness of the proto-city form.

The Nolli plan teaches us how to experience Rome. It invites us to see the city in terms of a reciprocal relationship of civic life to public space. In this sense it would not be incongruous to remark on the ambiguous exteriority of the interior architecture that characterises Borromini's first building, with its flowing colonnade of Corinthian columns and curving entablatures. The extraordinary facade was to

LEFT
Alvar Aalto, Savoy Vase and wood cast mould, 1936.

Space, Volume, Structure

be his final work, completed some years after his death. Being inside the church of San Carlino is like standing in a courtyard burrowed out of the urban block, its walls speaking the same language as the adjacent narrow cloister and the adjoining later facade. The interior volume behaves as if it were outdoors, an inside-outside space, integral to the larger spatial structure of the city. Borromini flattened out the traditional Greek cross plan to reduce any undue emphasis on the four ends of its axial arms. The street entry porch, three altars, two side chapels, the sacristy doorway and one window to the winding stair are stretched out between 16 columns, then pulled together to form a continuous serpentine screen. A single window, deeply inset over the door to the street, admits direct sunlight to shine through a golden railing and slice along the horizontal axis of the plan. However, the spatial emphasis is on the vertical axis, four levels stacked above one another, leading to the cupola lantern. The elliptical plan is squeezed from the sides to extend the perceived distance between altar and entrance. Each of eight focal points are centred exactly on alternately convex and concave planes of the lining walls. Straight lines of black stone set into the floor provide a rectilinear frame against which to register the visual movement of the wavy wall. And these thin black floorlines remind us of the drawing-board origins of the spatial geometry, of the squares and circles and diagonal lines that underlie all this undulation.

Like Aalto, whose surname in Finnish means 'wave', Borromini was known for his soft pencil drawings. Although there is no explicit geometrical skeleton beneath the wavy lines of the Savoy Vase, comparing these compatible vessels, wavy church and wavy vase, allows us to appreciate the world of one architect speaking to us through the work of another. Much of Siza's work, including his masterly and somewhat semi-wavy church of Marco de Canaveses, plays with a similar delamination of the soft layers of inner volumes from the hard crust of their outer shells.

We were introduced to Louis Kahn's first principles of architecture in our first-year studio at UCD. We did not realise how much we were learning by listening to what our tutor had himself recently learned from Kahn. One year later Kahn himself came to Dublin. He gave a memorable lecture at the Carroll's building on the Grand Canal. We found it not at all surprising to hear the substance of what he was whispering, about a brick's expectations with regard to an architect's intentions, more surprising to witness at first hand the chain of influence running from master through tutor to student. Shane de Blacam had not set us standard exercises, nor did he pose problems to which he held Kahnian solutions. With fundamentalist fervour, and using Kahn's guiding philosophy, he had encouraged us to experiment in a free spirit of enquiry. We have benefitted from the legacy of this first-year formative experience and have never shaken it off.

Kahn's writing remains hard to read, his buildings are difficult to deal with, their solemn monumentality sometimes in comical contrast to the quotidian conditions of American culture. Nevertheless, Kahn's buildings calmly stand their ground and hold their place in a quiet way that must be seen to be understood. Kimbell Arts Centre was itself alone worth a transatlantic trip to Texas. The first Kahn plan we studied was the Escherick House. Nearly 40 years later, while teaching at

ABOVE
Irish Language Cultural Centre, 2009, O'Donnell+Tuomey, watercolour sketch.

the University of Pennsylvania, I had the satisfaction of spending a morning at the house and most of the later afternoon in the archive, leafing through the portfolio of working drawings. I could compare my experience of the architecture with the documentation of its design. Kahn designed this house in 1959, the same year he visited Ronchamp. Not only its studio section but also the surface tension of its tautly stuccoed elevational scheme shows signs of the influence of Le Corbusier. Walking between the shelves of the archive, I was shown a drawing of the interior of Ronchamp, sketched on a detour taken from the Otterlo conference. Admittedly, the chapel looks a little squared off in this perspective, but Kahn once confessed, to Anne Tyng's ready disapproval, that he was "completely in love with Le Corbusier"— and, in the Escherick house, it shows.

From time to time, over mid-term breaks across the past 30 years, we've turned up to take the tour of some of Kahn's American monuments. We've puzzled over the practical problem of the Salk's reflective symmetry, tried to identify the entrance on the elevations of the Exeter library or to find something to soothe the echoing emptiness of its interior void, crossed the street from the experimental edginess of the Yale Art Gallery to the domestic interiority of the Mellon Centre, most regrettably missed the train to Trenton, marvelled at the improbable complexity of the cutaway corners in the Richards Laboratory. The Kimball is, as everybody knows, serene, sublime and simply perfect. You know you are within strong architecture. The critic is silenced. But the houses proved themselves a little more accessible to architects accustomed to working in an imperfect world.

LEFT
Academic Bookshop, Alvar Aalto.

RIGHT
San Carlo alle Quattro Fontana, interior volume.

Space, Volume, Structure

The Escherick House was finished in 1961. It was sensitively designed to suit its client, Margaret Escherick, a bookshop owner, niece of a renowned furniture maker, and sister of a California-based architect who had recommended her to Kahn. The blind wall of the living-room studio is treated as a thick wall of books, with a slit window cut down through the bookcase from the clerestory above. The additional thickness permits some play with the position of windows in the depth of the wall. This house took Kahn more than three years from design to construction, his office costs amounting to several multiples of the fees. Tragically, Margaret Escherick lived for only six months after its completion. In his subsequent house design for the Fishers, which took seven years from design to completion, Kahn's served-and-servant diagram was divided between living and sleeping. In the Escherick, the servant space subtly swallows almost everything that could be said to serve the studio living space. The separating zone of the stairhall stitches things together in between. Downstairs, the dining room is active on the garden side. Upstairs, the master bedroom straddles the scheme from front to back. If windows are the eyes of a house, then, in this

LEFT
Louis Kahn working on Fisher House design, 1961.

RIGHT
Louis Kahn, Fisher House, 1967, hinged space.

house, these eyes are the windows to its soul. The Escherick windows hold tight to the stretched surface of the outer skin, reflecting the light like vertical pools, reminding us that all glass once was liquid. The same windows exploit the depth of the bookwall, slicing dark shadows that make the hollow box of the house seem solid and deep. The chimney cleaves a window of its own, claiming its central position in the scheme. And at a smaller scale, the windows are put to work as mechanical contraptions, with various shutterboxes to control light and air. All this sophistication becomes more clearly legible on closer inspection of an apparently modest, poetically restrained plan.

The Fisher house is severely sectioned off from within itself into two parts, living and sleeping, and these halved parts are themselves hinged away or joined together in a way that holds their distance. Apart from the detail of the entrance hall in-between space, the bedroom block is not mysterious. The living room, skewered by a strange stone chimney stack rising out of the basement at its own skew to the plan, is a wonderful place, with its world-famous window. On the day when we were visiting, window cleaners were at work, moving like spiders across the inside and outside of the house with delicate care and nimble dexterity. Dr Fisher took us down to his basement workshop where he showed us the equipment for his regular house-maintenance regime. Kahn would have preferred the wooden cladding to have weathered with age. The Fishers liked it looking new. So, to prevent the house turning grey, as the architect would have wanted, or worse, to watch it patchily blackening behind the inevitable cracks in a varnished surface treatment, Dr Fisher agreed to painstakingly sand and seal the timber at annual intervals. And so the wood kept its

colour. As a compromise to his client's fastidious requirements, he told us, Kahn had increased the specified thickness of the cedar cladding, generously allowing for its gradual reduction by routine shaving. And the Fishers had loyally kept to their own and much more onerous side of the deal.

These two Kahn houses, the Fisher, when it was still happily lived in and lovingly maintained, and the Escherick, at the time of our visit, standing empty and on offer for sale, provided practical and intimate lessons in how to make a plan feel fresh and a section feel light, to make a building feel new and deeply archaic, all at the same time.

ABOVE
Escherick House, 1961, Louis Kahn.

Space, Volume, Structure

It's always interesting to visit a lived-in house while the original client is still in residence. We met Mrs Palmer at Frank Lloyd Wright's madly triangulated house in the trees, purpose-built for the Palmers in 1952. The house culminates in a triangular terrace, with built-in linen-covered couches, projecting high up in the tree canopy. Every element of the interior remained intact, even if it was worn and broken, as in this case, on that day, the underfloor heating. A bird-like woman of spartan refinement, Mrs Palmer told us she was reluctant to break up the red concrete floor, and so she chose to endure the considerable cold of a Michigan winter, reliant only on Wright's wide-open wood-burning fireplace. We realised that the dining table, the shower and, yes indeed, even the double bed, had been trapezoidally shaped and chamfered to fit the insistent geometry. Mrs Palmer explained that her husband, being the taller, had taken the longer side of the bed. And no, they had not bought any new piece of furniture in the 50 years since the house was completed, replying that "Mr Wright was kind of particular about his furniture!" This reminded me of an earlier time, visiting Yale with our late friend the brilliant Kevin Kieran, when we were asked by the gallery guard to leave an FLW furniture exhibition for laughing out loud at some of Mr Wright's more ludricrous chairs.

Useful Beauty History is not fixed or frozen in linear time. It is seen and told from different points of view. Architects develop their understanding by long, hard looking at actual buildings, seeing them with a sense of purpose, drawing details in their notebooks, drawing lessons from their observations, fixing them in their mind's eye. We can follow merging streams of thought and notice ideas as they emerge from different sources. Such confluential thinking is what Venturi describes as the "complex intricacies" of plan and section, the small wonders he discovered in his studies in Rome and later published to such powerful effect in *Complexity and Contradiction in Architecture*. There is so much to learn. We need to be able to read the background behind buildings and train ourselves to fluency in the tools of the trade. We have to internalise the archetypes that give continuity to the inherited culture. These things being registered, with due deference to the demands of a strict discipline, something else, something other, needs to happen to bring our buildings to sensible life, to unlock the latent potential of a given situation, to connect the definite act of building to the imperfect conditions of an uncertain world. Aalto tells us that "you can't save the world, you can only set it an example". We aspire to an architecture of useful beauty, an architecture that communicates, an active participant in the human conversation.

OPPOSITE
Early medieval oratory dedicated to St Matthias, Inishnee, Connemara.

+ Tribute

Dennis Gilbert died in June 2021.

The first time we met him, he came to photograph the Hudson house on site. The images he then captured on that grey and rainy day document a delicate stage in the construction, an empty concrete shell, but they also seemed to predict a future life for the structure as a ruin. He took five days to find fifteen photos of the Furniture College Letterfrack. He had fun with friends at the Photographers' Gallery recreating Hopper's *Nighthawks* in the corner cafe window. Across the past twenty-five years he had photographed almost all of the work of O'Donnell + Tuomey.

Dennis looked like Giacometti's *Walking Man*, moved like the master swordsman in *The Seven Samurai*, could fold his skinny legs like Coburn in *The Magnificent Seven*. He was exceptionally tall, tall by any standards and, head hidden under the darkcloth, beside the long black legs of his tripod, he stood like a stick insect. Like this he would stand still and silent, waiting for the cloud to pass, for the light to come along, motionless as a heron waiting for a fish. He was never known to be in a hurry, although sometimes to be seen caught in a sweat, whether from carrying his heavy equipment or caused by the heat of his concentration. Dennis didn't need to ask questions; he could read the work, interpret it in calm compositions. Whenever he needed to speak, it came out in a slow and hesitant drawl. I'd say – *you ok, Dennis?* He'd say – *I'm ok, John, just getting to grips with this bit of your geometry*. Or – *It's a good photo, but it's not your architecture; let's keep trying*. Or, finally, after a long time waiting – *Ok, I think that's it, we've got the duck's eye*.

The Hudson house—its three crucial elements: cave, court and tower seen here in their raw state—marks a point in the progress of our practice, a pilot fish for a school of projects to come.

LEFT
Hudson House, concrete shell.

RIGHT
Dennis Gilbert.

OPPOSITE
Hudson House, concrete shell.

Selected Works 2015–2021

We would like to acknowledge the commitment and creative contribution of the architects who worked with us on the projects selected for this book.

1999–2015 **ST ANGELA'S COLLEGE, CORK** Jeana Gearty (associate), Henrik Wolterstorff (project architect), Jitka Leonard, Sarah-Jane McGee, Paul Durcan, Peter Carroll.

2006–2018 **CAVANAGH BRIDGE, UNIVERSITY COLLEGE CORK** Willie Carey (associate director), Henrik Wolterstorff (project architect), Eoghan Horgan.

2011–2016 **CENTRAL EUROPEAN UNIVERSITY BUDAPEST (WITH TEAMPANNON/MATÉ HIDASNEMETI)** Mark Grehan (associate / project architect), Brian Barber, Anne Louise Duignan, Jitka Leonard, Kevin O'Brien, Ciara Reddy, Geoff Brouder, Henrik Wolterstorff, Jonathan Janssens, Iseult O'Clery, Donn Holohan, Edin Gicevic, Lauren Small, Gary Watkin.

2012 **FALLING DANSU, WRITING BUREAU (WITH JOSEPH WALSH STUDIO)**.

2012 **VESSEL (WITH JOSEPH WALSH STUDIO)** Brian Barber, Iseult O'Clery.

2013–2018 **SUNDAY'S WELL HOUSES, CORK** Willie Carey (director), Eoghan Horgan (project architect), Henrik Wolterstorff, Jitka Leonard, Anne Louise Duignan.

2014–2020 **STUDENT HUB, UNIVERSITY COLLEGE CORK** Willie Carey (director), Henrik Wolterstorff (associate), Eoghan Horgan, Minesh Patel, Darragh Collins, Jitka Leonard, Miguel Guerra Martínez, James Corboy, Cillian Briody, Clément Viroulaud, Hannah Wilson.

2015–2023 **CHRISTIAN BROTHERS COLLEGE, CORK** Willie Carey (director), Henrik Wolterstorff, Jitka Leonard (associates), Niall Crowley (project architect), Robert McCluskey, Hugh Ivers, Kylie Braithwaite, David Williams.

2015–2023 **V&A EAST, LONDON** Mark Grehan (director), Eimear Hanratty (associate director), Brian Barber, Kevin O'Brien (project architects), Anne Louise Duignan, Cormac Friel, David Williams, Laura Cannon, Laura Doyle, Darragh Farrell, Joyce Chen, Cameron Clarke, Ross Ledsham, James Barry, Yuqi Tang, Nigel Wynne, James Corboy, Finn Wilkie, Olwyn Greene, TJ Hartnett.

2015–2023 **SADLER'S WELLS DANCE THEATRE AND STUDIOS, LONDON** Jeana Gearty (director), Eimear Hanratty (associate director), Andrew Walsh (associate), Kate Griffin (project architect), Darragh Collins, Kylie Braithwaite, Eleanor Figueiredo, Eoghan Smith, Christian Smith, Ciara Reddy, Miguel Guerra Martínez, James Barry, Hannah Wilson, Finn Wilkie, Cameron Clarke, Joyce Chen, Olwyn Greene, TJ Hartnett.

2016–2023 **ACADEMIC HUB AND LIBRARY, TECHNOLOGICAL UNIVERSITY DUBLIN** Jeana Gearty (director), Darragh Collins, Denise Murray (associates), Andrew Walsh, Jitka Leonard (project architects), Ross Ledsham, Robert McCluskey, Hugh Ivers, Anthony McGinn, Kylie Braithwaite, Chester Kendell, Matthew Wilde, Clément Viroulaud, Hannah Wilson.

2016–2019 **SANDFORD PARK SCHOOLHOUSE, DUBLIN** Darragh Collins (associate), Jitka Leonard (project architect), Clément Viroulaud, Sam Holohan.

2016 **SHANGHAI GRAND OPERA HOUSE** Denise Murray (associate), Kevin O'Brien, Sam Holohan, Miguel Guerra Martínez, Kate Griffin, Cormac Friel, Andrew Walsh, Chester Kendell.

2016 **ROBINSON CENTRE, ROUNDSTONE** Cormac Friel, Kevin O'Brien, Cillian Briody, Emma Carroll.

2017 **THE PROW, LONDON** Eimear Hanratty (associate director), David Williams, Leroy Patterson, Cormac Friel, Johnny Poland, Cameron Clarke.

2018 **FUTURE CAMPUS, UNIVERSITY COLLEGE DUBLIN (WITH ALLIES AND MORRISON, PLATTENBAU STUDIO, SUPERPOSITION)** Willie Carey (director), Denise Murray (associate), David Williams, James Barry, Cormac Friel, Ross Ledsham, Leroy Patterson.

2018 **UNFINISHED MUSEUM (WITH JOSEPH WALSH STUDIO)** Brian Barber.

2018 **FOLDING LANDSCAPE/EAST AND WEST, VENICE BIENNALE** Brian Barber (project architect), Cormac Friel, James Barry, Brenda Sorohan, Martin Brennan, Henry Seward, John McGeady.

2018 **GRUNER + JAHR, HAMBURG** Denise Murray (associate), Henrik Wolterstorff (project architect), James Barry, Ross Ledsham, Christian Smith.

2019 **NIKOLAI INSEL, HAMBURG** Denise Murray (associate), Henrik Wolterstorff (project architect), James Barry, Ross Ledsham, Christian Smith.

2019 **WILLY BRANDT STRASSE, HAMBURG** Henrik Wolterstorff (project architect), James Barry, Ross Ledsham, Anthony McGinn.

2019–2023 **SCHOOL OF ARCHITECTURE, UNIVERSITY OF LIVERPOOL** Willie Carey (director), Henrik Wolterstorff (associate), James Barry (project architect), Ross Ledsham, Laura Doyle, Kevin O'Brien.

2020 **ALTERNATIVE HISTORIES, DRAWING MATTER EXHIBITION** Hugh Ivers.

2020 **CLONLIFFE APARTMENTS, DUBLIN** Jeana Gearty (director), Anne Louise Duignan (project architect), Ferdia Kenny, Cormac Friel, Jitka Leonard, Kevin O'Brien.

And we would also like to thank the following people for their patient help with making this particular book: Maeve Power and Brian Barber, our in-house editors; Anna Danby, Daphne Fordham-Smith at Artifice Press and, once again, Rachel Pfleger, book designer at Artifice Press.

Image Credits

9 **(TOP)** Sheila O'Donnell; 9 **(BOTTOM)** John Tuomey; 10 O'Donnell+Tuomey; 12 Millennium Models; 14 **(LEFT)** Ogic; 14 **(RIGHT)** Picture Plane; 17 Bruce Darrell; 19 **(TOP LEFT AND RIGHT)** Sheila O'Donnell; 19 **(BOTTOM LEFT)** John Tuomey; 19 **(BOTTOM RIGHT)** Mary Evans Picture Library © agefotostock; 21 Picture Plane; 22 **(LEFT)** Sheila O'Donnell; 22 **(RIGHT)** John Tuomey; 23 **(TOP LEFT)** Mary Evans Picture Library © agefotostock; 23 **(BOTTOM LEFT)** John Tuomey; 25 Picture Plane; 26 **(TOP)** Picture Plane; 27 **(TOP)** Picture Plane; 27 **(BOTTOM LEFT)** John Tuomey; 29 Picture Plane; 30 **(TOP LEFT)** Picture Plane; 30 **(TOP RIGHT)** John Tuomey; 30 **(BOTTOM)** Picture Plane; 32 **(TOP LEFT)** Staatsarchiv Hamburg, 720-3_1/B 0001; 32 **(TOP RIGHT)** Historical archive of Commerzbank; 32 **(BOTTOM)** Picture Plane; 34 **(BOTTOM LEFT)** Sheila O'Donnell; 34 **(BOTTOM RIGHT)** Picture Plane; 35 Picture Plane; 38 **(TOP)** O'Donnell+Tuomey/Allies and Morrison; 38 **(BOTTOM)** Sheila O'Donnell; 40 **(TOP)** Picture Plane; 41 Picture Plane; 44 **(RIGHT)** © Estate of Gordon Matta-Clark. ARS NY/IVARO Dublin, 2021. Courtesy David Zwirner; 49 **(RIGHT)** UCC Archives; 50 John Tuomey; 57 **(LEFT)** Sheila O'Donnell; 67 Sheila O'Donnell; 69 ZOA3D; 70 **(BOTTOM RIGHT)** John Tuomey; 71 **(TOP)** ZOA3D;

103 Picture Plane; 106 (TOP) C.H. Reilly, L.B. Budden, and J.E. Marshall, SPEC LUP.932.BUD, By Courtesy of the University of Liverpool Library; 107 (TOP) Picture Plane; 107 (BOTTOM) John Tuomey; 117 (TOP RIGHT) Forbes Massie; 118 (LEFT) Zaha Hadid, Drawing Matter Archive; 119 (TOP) John Tuomey; 119 (BOTTOM LEFT) Wiltshire Collection Image Courtesy of the National Library of Ireland; 129 (TOP) Bing Maps (Microsoft) 2011; 154-163 Sheila O'Donnell; 166 (TOP RIGHT) Sheila O'Donnell; 168 Sheila O'Donnell; 179 Picture Plane; 180 Picture Plane; 181 (BOTTOM LEFT) Sheila O'Donnell; 181 (TOP AND BOTTOM RIGHT) Picture Plane; 185 (LEFT) Mick O'Dea; 185 (RIGHT) Sheila O'Donnell/John Tuomey collection; 190 (TOP AND BOTTOM LEFT) Sheila O'Donnell; 190 (BOTTOM RIGHT) John Tuomey; 193 (BOTTOM) Sheila O'Donnell; 197 (BOTTOM LEFT) Sheila O'Donnell; 201 (LEFT) *The Architectural Review*, Issue 805; 201 (RIGHT) *Domus* magazine, November 1998; 204 (LEFT) John Tuomey; 205 John Tuomey; 206 O'Donnell+Tuomey/Allies and Morrison/Arquitecturia; 211 (TOP) O'Donnell+Tuomey/Allies and Morrison/Arquitecturia; 212 O'Donnell+Tuomey/Allies and Morrison/Arquitecturia; 217 (TOP) O'Donnell+Tuomey/Allies and Morrison/Arquitecturia; 217 (BOTTOM) John Tuomey; 218 Sheila O'Donnell; 220 Allies and Morrison; 225 (TOP) O'Donnell+Tuomey/Allies and Morrison/Arquitecturia; 227 O'Donnell+Tuomey/Allies and Morrison/Arquitecturia; 231 (TOP) O'Donnell+Tuomey/Ninety90; 232 O'Donnell+Tuomey/Ninety90; 243 Sheila O'Donnell; 244 Albertina, Vienna; 245 Martii Kapanen, Alvar Aalto Museum Archive; 246 Sheila O'Donnell; 248 (LEFT) Louis I. Kahn Collection © University of Pennsylvania and Pennsylvania Historical and Museum Commission. Photo by George Pohl.

Photographic Credits   HÉLÈNE BINET 241; BOURNE GROUP LTD 123 (left); ANDREW BRADLEY 114, 116 (left); TAMÁS BUJNOVSZKY 2, 53, 54 (left), 55, 57 (right), 58 (top), 60, 62, 63, 66 (right), back cover; WILLIE CAREY 136 (top right); ALICE CLANCY 49 (left), 54, 56, 61, 64, 65, 66 (left), 94, 110, 112, 113, 128, 129 (bottom), 136 (left and bottom right); WILL DIMOND 44 (left); JEANA GEARTY 124 (left); DENNIS GILBERT 47, 127, 130, 131 (top), 133, 134, 137, 138, 147, 148 (top and bottom), 150, 152 (top and bottom), 166 (left), 169, 172, 176, 182, 196, 199 (top right and bottom), 200, 238, 240, 252 (left), 253; DENNIS GILBERT/VIEW 252 (right); MARK GREHAN 51 (left); EIMEAR HANRATTY 122 (right), 123 (right); STE MURRAY front cover, 116 (right), 117 (top left), 195, 197 (right), 199 (top left); JED NIEZGODA 42, 73, 76, 78 (bottom), 79, 80 (top), 81, 82, 85, 86, 87 (top), 88, 91, 92, 96, 97, 98 (top), 99, 100, 143, 164, 171, 175; SHEILA O'DONNELL 203 (left); JOHN TUOMEY 4, 6–8, 13, 45, 46, 75 (top), 120, 122 (left), 124 (top right), 125, 165, 183, 184 (left), 186, 187 (left), 189, 234 (top), 239 (left and right), 247 (left and right), 249, 250; DANIEL VEGEL 51 (right), 124 (bottom right); WILLIAM WHITAKER 248 (right).

Biographies   Sheila O'Donnell and John Tuomey have worked together for more than 30 years. They have exhibited six times at the Venice Biennale. They have been seven times winners of the AAI Downes Medal, four times shortlisted for the RIBA International Prize, five times finalists for the RIBA Stirling Prize and finalists for the EU Mies Prize. They were recipients of the RIAI Gold Medal in 2005 and 2021, the highest award in Irish architecture. They were awarded the American Academy Brunner Prize and RIBA Royal Gold Medal for their contribution to international architecture. Professors at University College Dublin, they have lectured at architecture schools around the world. They are members of Aosdána, the affiliation of Irish artists. Sheila O'Donnell is a member of the American Academy of Arts and Letters. Previous publications include *Space for Architecture*, to which this book is a companion volume.

LEFT
John Tuomey + Sheila O'Donnell, Hungarian quarry.

Project Credits and Biographies

© 2022 SJH Group

This book is published by Artifice Press Limited, a company registered in England and Wales with company number 11182108. Artifice Press Limited is an imprint within the SJH Group. Copyright is owned by the SJH Group. All rights reserved.

Artifice Press Limited
The Maple Building
39–51 Highgate Road
London NW5 1RT
United Kingdom
—
+44 (0)20 8371 4047
office@artificeonline.com
www.artificeonline.com

Designed by Rachel Pfleger
Printed in Lithuania by Kopa

ISBN 978-1-911339-45-8

British Library in Cataloguing Data. A CIP record for this book is available from the British Library.

Neither this publication nor any part of it may be reproduced, stored in a retrieval system or transmitted in any form or by any means, electronic, mechanical, photocopying, recording or otherwise, without the prior permission of the SJH Group or the appropriately accredited copyright holder.

All information in this publication is verified to the best of the author's and publisher's ability. However, Artifice Press Limited and the SJH Group do not accept responsibility for any loss arising from reliance on it. Where opinion is expressed, it is that of the author and does not necessarily coincide with the editorial views of the publisher. The publishers have made all reasonable efforts to trace the copyright owners of the images reproduced herein, and to provide an appropriate acknowledgment in the book.

Also available:

Space for Architecture: The Work of O'Donnell+Tuomey
ISBN 978-1-908967-47-3

Saw Swee Hock: The Realisation of the London School of Economics Student Centre
ISBN 978-1-908967-52-7